Endorsements

A warm, winsome, and captivating forty-day journey to godly leadership.
—*Anne Graham Lotz, Founder and President, AnGeL Ministries*

While Shepherds Watch Their Flocks has superbly woven together Scripture's pastoral culture and its leadership themes, modeling for us the genuinely biblical leadership of our Chief Shepherd.
—*Leighton Ford, President, Leighton Ford Ministries and Honorary Life Chairman of the Lausanne Committee for World Evangelization*

Laniak's work has helped me see the shepherd image in an entirely new way. I am particularly struck by the way shepherding connects with peacemaking—it is vital for church leaders not only to have a shepherd's tender heart, but also to have the courage to protect and the wisdom to guide their flocks.
—*Ken Sande, Founder, Peacemaker Ministries and President, Relational Wisdom 360*

Through real-life stories of shepherds, Christian leaders are called to be not only tender and loving, but also tough and disciplined.
—*Dr. John M. Perkins, Founder and President, The John M. Perkins Foundation*

Of the leadership models in Jesus' ministry, only the servant has received in-depth treatment. Laniak's investigation into the shepherd model is desperately needed by today's leaders.
—*Dr. Bobby Clinton, Professor of Leadership, Fuller Theological Seminary*

A must read for those who desire to lead congregations and bring the essential values of the Kingdom beyond the parish to the world.
—*Rev. Marty McCarthy, Former Rector, Saint John's Episcopal Church, Charlotte, NC*

A spiritual quest that could have been written specifically for military chaplains.
—*Captain Jessie R. Tate, Former US Fleet Forces Command*

Accomplishing what few authors can, Laniak creates powerful images with fascinating stories, exegetical insights, and stunning photos, bringing biblical leadership to life for pastors and lay leaders alike.
—*Dr. James F. Cobble, Jr., Founder, Institute of Church Leadership*

More than an inspirational read, this book is a timely invitation into the shepherd's world which will compel you to reflect on your Christian life and leadership with a new sense of awe and assurance.
—*Dr. Barry Corey, President, Biola University*

In a day when leadership is often more about the leader than anyone else, Laniak's refreshing insights provide a roadmap for further reflection long after the 40 days of readings have been completed.
—*Dr. John Pellowe, CEO, Canadian Council of Christian Charities*

A unique blend of first hand cultural experiences, biblical insights, and contemporary applications.
—*Kirk Franklin, Executive Director, Wycliffe International*

Navy admirals, homemakers, layleaders, and church staff have all said the same thing, "I have learned not only how to more effectively serve in the church but also how to lead in every area of life."
—*Nate Atwood, Pastor, St. Giles Presbyterian Church and Moderator of the 29th Evangelical Presbyterian Church General Assembly*

Anyone entrusted with ministry responsibilities will be treated to exceptional leadership insights, welcome guidance, and rare encouragement to renew their passion for attending to the needs of God's flock.
—*Dr. Mark W. McCloskey, Lead Faculty, Transformational Leadership, Bethel Seminary*

Believing that the shepherding task flows from a heart of compassion and a clear sense of justice, Laniak reminds us of the people, priorities, purposes, and perseverance to which we are called.
—*Bishop Claude Alexander, Jr., Senior Pastor, The Park Ministries, Charlotte, NC*

While Shepherds Watch Their Flocks provides the delightful combination of readability, scholarship and usefulness. I highly recommend the book for everyone seeking to understand biblical leadership, especially for those involved in multi-cultural leadership.
—*Dr. James E. Plueddemann, Professor of Cross-Cultural Leadership,*
  Trinity Evangelical Divinity School, and Former International Director of SIM

Tim Laniak has brought so many fresh, helpful insights into shepherding, so much so that I gave copies of his magnificent book to each of our 21 elders and 14 program staff!
—*Dr. John Huffman, Former Senior Pastor, St. Andrews Presbyterian Church,*
  Newport Beach, CA; Board Chairman, Christianity Today International

More than a book on leadership theory, *While Shepherds Watch Their Flocks* is an invitation to undergo a cultivation process to become a biblical shepherd leader.
—*Lim K. Tham, General Secretary of the Bible Society in Singapore*

While Shepherds Watch Their Flocks combines accessible scholarship, captivating insights and an elegant lay-out to give any reader timeless leadership wisdom. Dr. Laniak's love for the Bible, love for the Land and love for shepherds (in the desert and in the Church) is compelling and contagious.
—*Dr. Garth Bolinder, Superintendent, Midsouth Conference, Evangelical*
  Covenant Church

Inspired by our Christian heritage and rooted in the Word of God, Laniak unpacks for his reader the reality of a shepherd's life in parallel to today's pastor and ministry leader.
—*Dr. Stephen A. Macchia, Founding President, Leadership Transformations, Inc.*

A welcome addition in a world scarce with mature theological reflection on the person and practice of the leader.
—*Dr. David Baer, President, Overseas Council*

While Shepherds Watch Their Flocks teaches us that biblical shepherding requires everything we've got, and nothing less.
—*Dr David Wong, Former V.P. for International Training, Haggai Institute Leadership*

The implications of the statement, "We are shepherds," needs to be grasped by those functioning at every level of Christian leadership, particularly those in administrative roles.
—*Commissioner John Busby, Retired National Commander, The Salvation Army*

While Shepherds Watch Their Flocks is a powerful tool for training small group leaders, helping making those intimate connections in this culture of huge flocks and few shepherds.
—*Dr. Jan Kempe, President, Faithful Hearts, Raleigh-Durham, NC*

A refreshing devotional that draws the long time Christian leader back to first base... and equally equips the new pastor, elder or deacon who desires to remain faithful over the long haul.
—*Dr. David Yap, Pastor, Yio Chu Kang Chapel, Singapore and Chairman, SIM East Asia*

A breath of fresh air for pastors and lay leaders alike. I'm recommending it as must reading for all my students!
—*Dr. S. Donald Fortson, Associate Professor of Church History and Practical Theology, Reformed Theological Seminary*

We gifted every leader in our church with this profound and accessible book, thoroughly bathing our imagination and practice of leadership through the primary lens of shepherd. This is the right tool to reassert biblical rather than business concepts at the heart of Christian leadership.
—*Rev. Dr. Mike Moses, Lead Pastor, Lake Forest Church, Huntersville, NC; Church Planter and Church Planting Coach, Evangelical Presbyterian Church*

Forward

Those of us in leadership today like to think of ourselves as "shepherds," but we may have created shepherds in our own image. Tim Laniak agrees that, as Christian leaders, we should think of ourselves as shepherds, but he brings to our identity an unsettling biblical and cultural realism. Shepherding a flock in the Near East has always been demanding and often demeaning work, and it took all a person could give to do it well. Laniak, Dean and Professor of Old Testament at Gordon-Conwell Seminary, has spent a portion of his life researching shepherds up close and personal, and in the following pages he guides the reader to appreciate—and embrace—all that biblical shepherding involves.

Almost forty years ago Philip Keller wrote a soul-opening book, *A Shepherd Looks at Psalm 23*. The journey in the following pages will take you beyond that devotional classic. With insightful words and splendid photographs, Laniak brings both a scholar's mind and a pastor's heart to his writing. Elders and deacons, pastors, parents and seminary presidents are correct in regarding themselves as shepherds. *While Shepherds Watch Their Flocks* raises our job description to a divine standard.

—*Dr. Haddon W. Robinson, Former President,
Gordon-Conwell Theological Seminary*

About the Author

Tim Laniak made his first trip to the Middle East in 1977 and has enjoyed opening up the history and cultures of the biblical world to students and leaders ever since. He and his wife Maureen have lived in Israel and occasionally guide study tours to the region. This book contains insights gleaned primarily from a year of field research while on sabbatical from Gordon-Conwell Theological Seminary (Charlotte, North Carolina) where Tim serves as Dean, Professor of Old Testament, and Mentor for the Christian Leadership Doctor of Ministry Program.

Laniak (Th.D., Harvard University) has authored several books including *Shepherds After My Own Heart: Pastoral Traditions and Leadership in the Bible, Shame and Honor in the Book of Esther,* the New International Biblical Commentary on the book of Esther, and *Handbook for Hebrew Exegesis.* Visit his web site at www.ShepherdLeader.com.

WHILE SHEPHERDS WATCH THEIR FLOCKS

Forty Daily Reflections on Biblical Leadership

Dr. Timothy S. Laniak

Photography by David Ormesher

ShepherdLeader Publications
www.ShepherdLeader.com

Dedicated respectfully to Dr. Robert E. Cooley,
a model shepherd who brings the highest level of scholarship
in Bible and Anthropology
to his understanding and practice of Christian leadership

Table of Contents

Acknowledgments

This book is the result of generosity from two institutions and countless individuals. Funding for my field research came from the Trustees of Gordon-Conwell Theological Seminary who provided me with a sabbatical in 2003–04. During that year the Trustees of the Albright Institute for Archaeological Research in Jerusalem supported my work as their Annual Professor. I feel deeply indebted to the many shepherds, mostly Bedouin, who "took me into their tents" and opened up their lives to me. They've honored me with trust to tell their stories to the world. My translator, Sáte, was a gracious host through many long days of interviewing, offering not only his time but his friendship for life. May God grant him and his new bride many children and large flocks.

I want to thank a team of specialists who have contributed to this book and related resources. My long time friend Dave Ormesher took time off from his company in Chicago to share an adventure and get back behind a camera. Photos were also contributed graciously by Todd Bolen (www.bibleplaces.com), Jim Martin, Matt Doll, and other accommodating friends. I can't express my gratitude enough to editors Janet Thoma and Tabitha Plueddemann, midwives who helped me give birth to forty chapters that each came with labor pains. Layout was designed and executed superbly by Carl Etzel, artist extraordinaire, and Tyler Gordon, source of our daily pdfs—two men who proved patient with an author who found it too easy to ask, "What if we tried...?" Many thanks to Tina and Jeremy Long who helped with image treatments and to Trish King and my mother, Jane Laniak, for proof reading.

I am indebted especially to three of the many spiritual shepherds who read early versions of the manuscript, took it seriously, and gave incisive feedback: Bob Thompson, Jamie Walters, and Tamara Park. Bob and Jamie continued working with the book after I was finished, organizing the discussion that led to the forums in "The Tent" at www.ShepherdLeader.com.

My appreciation runs deepest for my family. Our "kids," Jesse and Adrienne, were great travelers (even on cranky camels) and joined in the fun of interviewing. Adrienne still reminds me that I needed her to translate for me. Jesse may regret turning down an offer to become a Bedouin someday. Aaron was studying back in the U.S.—never able to explain to his friends why Dad spent a year with sheep and goats! My incredible wife Maureen—model shepherd, partner in ministry, and my fellow sojourner in green pastures and dark valleys for more than thirty years—has supported this project from its inception, as she has all of my endeavors. Her value, as my Bedouin friends would say, is greater than a thousand camels.

We are the people of his pasture,
the flock under his care.

—Psalm 95:7

Introduction

"Hey Mister!, what is there to research about us? We are nothing! Just spend our lives running after sheep and goats. Neither home, nor an address. Sleeping under the open sky, in winter, summer, and rains... Year after year we measure the length of roads by our feet, carrying cooking utensils on camels and mules. Can't even rest in one place for a week. Why waste time, then, yours and ours?"[1]

These are the words of young shepherds trying to make sense of an outsider studying their way of life. They find their own lives marginal and enigmatic, so why study them? Paradoxically, here on the fringes of society, a marginalized vocation older than civilization holds the key to understanding leadership in our own day. Not just leadership generally, but *biblical* leadership.

The following pages provide personal access into the lives of real shepherds. Shepherds from many countries across the Middle East and beyond. Shepherds from many historical periods.[2] The kinds of shepherds the Bible makes much of. This book came as the result of my own personal journey into these lives, searching for the context and meaning of the persistent pastoral imagery in Scripture. I wanted firsthand exposure to the cultural fabric of this central metaphor chosen to convey profound and timeless truths about leadership.

The opportunity came during the academic year 2003–04 when I took a sabbatical at the Albright Institute for Archaeological Research in Jerusalem. Mixing library research with field interviews in Israel, Jordan, and the Sinai, I began to unlock the metaphor that has enlightened the work of leaders for millennia. I grew to love the deserts and wildernesses where Bedouin[3] tribes raise their flocks. I am indebted to so many for taking me into their tents and opening up their worlds to me. Their comments on the common everyday world of shepherd work began to shape my understanding of biblical passages on leadership in unexpected ways.

Returning to my work of training shepherds for the church, I found an eager audience for these images and insights and their implications for contemporary ministry. Though some have their doubts, I am convinced more than ever that the shepherd metaphor needs to be reinvigorated rather than replaced.

Through this book I invite fellow Christian leaders to trek into the wilderness and reflect together on our lives and work as shepherds. Seize this opportunity to reflect on your Divine Shepherd and your calling as his field hand. Ideally, set aside forty days for this personal journey. We'll begin each day with a brief chapter, each a collage of photographic images, excerpts from interviews, scriptural insights, and thought-provoking questions. Let this book guide your personal sojourn in the wilderness.

Forty is a significant number in the Bible, especially in desert settings. Moses spent forty days fasting on top of Mt. Sinai while God wrote out the sacred charter for his people.[a] Israel spent forty years in a desolate wilderness, deprived of life's basics so that they might learn dependence on God and his word. Forty years in an environment intentionally chosen by God to reveal his will and character—and to shape human will and character. Jesus spent forty days at the beginning of his ministry in a wilderness. Forty days in fasting and solitary prayerful reflection. Perhaps you might choose to fast in some way during this period.

The wilderness is where God revealed himself repeatedly as *Provider*, *Protector*, and *Guide*. These three primary roles of a shepherd will organize the overall structure of our reflections. You'll find thirteen chapters devoted to each.

The chapters begin with *Observations* (marked by the staff symbol) about some aspect of traditional shepherd life, continue with *Investigations* (marked by the scroll symbol) into related Bible passages, and conclude with *Implications* (marked by the sandal symbol)—questions and contemporary scenarios for our continued reflection. You will undoubtedly generate other insights and questions of your own. Record these in "The Tent" at www.ShepherdLeader.com or keep a written journal, detailing applications for your own ministry setting.

Although this book has obvious and direct relevance for pastors and elders, I often use the terms *leader* and *community* to avoid restricting the implications to

---

a. Exod. 34:28

congregational life. Believers who serve in positions of responsibility in any setting should find the content relevant. Because organized or unorganized, large or small, every group is a community. And every community has leaders. And all leaders are shepherds. Pastors and politicians. Corporate executives and stay-at-home parents. Chaplains and coaches. Teachers and hospice workers. Construction supervisors and county commissioners. Virtually all of us are shepherds, responsible to God for the way we lead those in our care. Pastors should be thinking of their congregations not only as sheep (and goats!), but also as shepherds working among their own flocks.

My own experience as a shepherd includes a wide variety of venues. I've led children's clubs, youth groups, neighborhood Bible studies, and evangelistic outreaches. I've managed a home for international students and welfare housing for elderly immigrants. I've started non-profit organizations and served on their boards. I've taught in the U.S., Europe, and Asia, serving with para-church organizations, denominations, and local churches. Over the last fifteen years I've been training students in a seminary setting, marveling at the amazing diversity of communities to which God has called shepherd leaders. I must admit that the most challenging setting for my own shepherding has been at home. The implications in this book very often confronted me first quite personally in the context of my marriage and family life.

In the pages that follow, you will not simply be soothed by inspirational thoughts and pictures of pastoral scenes. The Bible does not offer the shepherd metaphor as an exercise in literary artistry, but rather to teach about leadership. Divine leadership and human leadership. In fact, shepherd imagery is used mostly in critiques of poor human leadership. The verbal pictures—grounded in cultural realities—help create an inescapable standard for responsible leadership. These pictures spoke to the original readers in the most serious terms. Like parables, metaphors compel a person to think, to feel, and to act differently. The metaphor of the shepherd leader still makes its comprehensive challenge today. Please join me in embracing this challenge.

As a bride you loved me and followed
me through the desert.

—Jeremiah 2:2

The Wilderness

Our first impression of deserts and wilderness is visual monotony. Shadows crawl across the stone-strewn valleys. The sand-colored terrain is bleached in searing sunlight. Only after settling into its unhurried rhythm will you recognize subtle, continuous changes. Scattered vegetation surfaces around hidden moisture sources. Animals that hide during the day emerge at dusk. The star-studded night highlights surreal contours in the landscape. In time you become mesmerized by the vast and barren grandeur.

While a desert landscape can lure the newcomer into a romantic trance, we soon discover that this environment is fierce and inhospitable, known for drastic extremes. Its heat can overwhelm, as I once learned dramatically. In 1977 our team of four left Jerusalem before dawn to hike to a remote monastery in the Judean Wilderness. Our chosen route would be the Kidron Valley, the setting for the Good Samaritan story. It was a blistering July morning, and by 10 a.m. I was dehydrated in nature's furnace. "There was fire around, and fire beneath, and overhead the sun."[1] Our water bottles were empty. The oranges were finished. So were we. *Khalas*, in Arabic. Finished. The Bedouin say, "The pail of thirst has no rope."[2]

Arriving in the suffocating heat with a full-blown migraine, I collapsed in the shade of the monastery's entryway. My only hope to get out was a *sherut* (contract taxi) that pulled in at noon. Packed with French tourists with a roundtrip fare, there was no room for a sick hiker. I pleaded for space—even in the trunk. And one hour later I rode out, slung over their bags, holding the trunk open, gasping for air. The temperature was a piping 125 degrees Fahrenheit.

Unbelievably, desert temperatures may drop over 80 degrees in the dead of a winter. The furnace becomes a freezer. Restless and shivering, tent dwellers stoke their fires through sleepless nights. At dawn, shepherds wonder what they've surrendered to the icy darkness. In the severe winter of 1945–46, nomads of Algeria lost half of their herds to freezing. A sober bystander recalls a similar tragedy in Palestine: "I still remember how those poor sheep...died in dozens while their owners stood looking at them, unable to do anything for them."[3] The desert is a place of death.

Temperature changes are bearable, but not when accompanied by the desert's most dreaded plague—*drought*. Years may pass with only drops of dew for moisture. In the territories of the Bedouin, adequate rain may fall on an average of three years in ten. Between 1958 and 1961 Syria lost 50 percent of its sheep and 85 percent of its camels to rainless winters. One poet pines,

> Singed by the flames of a hot breeze from the south...
> Emaciated animals in a drought-stricken land.
> The flames of the blistering heat are licking their hearts;
> They have nothing to eat, except charred branches of the
> > *wahat* tree.[4]

Hamsin is another capricious seasonal phenomenon. This dreaded sand hurricane can blow through a camp for days, decimating any unprotected life. "You see fine specks of soil surging and colliding together, grains and specks that lash the face like a whip, parch the throat, and sap the strength of one's soul. The rising dust blinds the eyes, and the animals wander in lost confusion."[5]

The landscape heightens the danger by its deceptive capacity to look both familiar and unfamiliar at every turn. One can get lost just minutes from the tents or wander far from home and never know it.

The wilderness is featured in many biblical narratives. The Sinai Peninsula, the Negev, and the Wildernesses of Zin, Paran, and Judah are arid zones where fugitives like Moses and David fled, and where Jesus escaped to pray.

Yet even the most desolate desert offered a spiritual oasis for calling, revelation, and intimacy. The root of the Hebrew word for wilderness, *midbar*, means "word."

After four decades of trudging in this rugged terrain, the shepherd Moses met God on his sacred mountain home.[6] Moses was summoned to bring Israel out of slavery from Egypt's oppressive society back to this remote mountain where God would give his people words of life.

After receiving the Torah, Moses shepherded God's human flock for forty years in the wild Negev where dependence on God was imperative.

> Remember how the LORD your God led you all the way in the
> desert these forty years...He humbled you, causing you to hunger
> and then feeding you with manna...to teach you that man does not
> live on bread alone but on every word that comes from the mouth
> of the LORD. (Deut. 8:2–3)

The prophet Hosea understood that God deliberately "lured" his people into desert regions where he "proposed" to them.[a] Only in this remote, isolated

---

a. Hosea 2:14

environment would they be able to comprehend his love for them—and their desperate need for him.

The ministry of Jesus was inaugurated with a display of divine affirmation at the Jordan River. The Holy Spirit descended on him like a dove, but then abruptly led him into the wilderness to endure severe temptation. Symbolically, Jesus relived the challenge that God's people had once failed. Matching their forty years, Jesus spent forty days sustained exclusively by God's word. Biblically, the wilderness is a place of dependent, disciplined, purifying solitude where God must be trusted. Deserts bring people quickly to the end of their self-sufficiency and independence.

The wilderness is also associated with wild expectations. It is the *tohu wavohu* ("formlessness and void")[7] into which God speaks a new creation. The prophetic promises for a dramatic renewal of exiled Israel were framed by images of a flower-carpeted desert coursing with rushing streams of living water. Jesus' ministry paved a "way in the wilderness,"[a] a spiritually barren landscape where threatened and thirsty people panted for a new Eden.

a. Isa. 40:3

Our lives can become a wilderness when experiences expose our frail and tenuous existence. Episodes of bewilderment, abandonment, and inner terror reveal our soul's restless cravings and fundamental neediness.

In the wilderness we can lose our bearings.

Or regain them.

The wilderness can be such a catalyst for good, we may voluntarily create one for the purpose of recharging our relationship with God. We can block out the calendar and unplug the technological gadgets for some uninterrupted time in a setting that isolates us in his presence. This journal could reflect a deliberate, intentional choice to meet with God.

Let's prepare for our journey by expecting God to reveal his word, to provide insight into our souls, and to purge us spiritually in this divinely chosen furnace. We need to leave our "stuff" behind, removing every distraction, and prepare for stillness. God will honor our choice to meet him alone in the wilderness during these forty days.

PROVISION

Then I will give you shepherds after my own heart,
who will lead you with knowledge and understanding.

—Jeremiah 3:15

PROVISION

During the course of interviews in Jordan, Israel, and the Sinai, I asked as many open-ended questions as possible. I didn't want my preconceived ideas of shepherding to influence my research. One of my common questions was, "What does it take to be a shepherd?"

I heard many answers, some of which I'll share in the chapters ahead. Khaled said you had to grow up in a shepherding family. Others suggested that I might be able to catch on in a few months if I worked for an owner who would supervise my work. No one had a curriculum. Just long-term apprenticeship.

One of the most memorable responses came from a Jordanian Bedouin, Abu-Jamal. Sitting together in his tent, he contemplated before answering. "What really matters is that you have the *heart* for it. If you do, you can begin tomorrow." He then looked me straight in the eye and said, "I think you have the heart for it."

I thanked him for the compliment, wondering if it was more than flattery.

A moment later Abu-Jamal indulged in some personal grief and then paid another compliment. My thirteen-year-old son Jesse had started this conversation with us, politely sipped some of the coffee, and studied the Kalashnikov rifle hanging in the tent. But by now he was out playing with the flocks. Abu-Jamal spoke as one father to another. "My sons don't have the heart for this work so they don't deserve the business. I'll sell the flocks to someone else before I let my sheep go to those who don't care for them."

Then he looked me in the eye again and said, "Your son has the heart for the animals. I can see it. You tell him that he can come stay with me. I'll give him two hundred sheep, a wife, and a good Jordanian education in any school he wants."

The image of Jesse as a Jordanian shepherd was amusing, but Abu-Jamal didn't seem to be joking. "You ask Jesse to think about it and give me an answer tomorrow."

Jesse was surprised by the offer and seemed wary about the details. Having eyed one of the young daughters who might be in the deal, he politely refused when asked. Abu-Jamal understood, but he made us promise "on our nose" to come for a feast when we returned to the country. I gave him the suggested signal as we headed back to the car.

I'll never know how serious my Bedouin friend's offer was, but I'll always remember how he valued a shepherd's heart.

Abu-Jamal's comments remind me of the proverb, "A righteous man *cares* for the needs of his animal."[a] The Bedouin's perspective began to illuminate other Scriptures for me as well.

After centuries of leadership failure in the Old

Testament period, God promised Israel through Jeremiah that he would give them "shepherds after my own heart."[a] God watched the community's leaders and, like my Bedouin host, decided that they did not deserve the "family business" because they didn't have the Owner's heart. God's anger surfaced again in Zechariah's preaching because "their own shepherds take no compassion on them."[b]

In Ezekiel divine condemnation for the leaders is piercing, while compassion for the flock is transparent:

> Woe to the shepherds of Israel who only take care of themselves! Should not shepherds take care of the flock? You eat the curds, clothe yourselves with the wool and slaughter the choice animals, but you do not take care of the flock. You have not strengthened the weak or healed the sick or bound up the injured. You have not brought back the strays or searched for the lost. (Ezek. 34:2–4)

Ezekiel then promised that God would come personally to care for his flock.

Jesus came as God in the flesh, expressing his shepherd love to a leaderless community. "When he saw the crowds, he had compassion on them, because they were harassed and helpless, like sheep without a shepherd."[c] Compassion prompted his healing and deliverance ministry as well as his teaching.

The compassionate concerns of the Good Shepherd were caught by his followers. Paul said the "*care* of all the churches" was his greatest burden.[d] In the pastoral epistles he commends Timothy by saying, "I have no one else like him, who takes a *genuine interest in your welfare*."[e] Paul urges his colleagues in ministry to "*encourage* the timid, *help* the weak, *be patient* with everyone."[f] Work for the Chief Shepherd, Peter insists, requires an *eagerness to serve*.[g] The desire to serve

---

a. Jer. 3:15 b. Zech. 11:5 (author's translation) c. Matt. 9:36 d. 2 Cor. 11:28 (KJV) e. Phil. 2:20
f. 1 Thess. 5:14 g. 1 Pet. 5:2

and nurture is expected of every husband: "Husbands, love your wives, just as Christ loved the church and gave himself up for her."[a]

The caring aspects of spiritual shepherding in Scripture are best exemplified in the roles of the priests. Though we primarily remember Israel's ancient clergy as animal slaughterers, they were the community's religious caregivers. They helped their fellow believers access God's presence and announced his forgiveness. They discerned God's will, led God's people in worship, and taught the Torah. Priests were reconcilers, dispensers of God's grace in concrete and tangible ways. In Hebrews 2:17–18 the writer describes Christ as a merciful priest who was willing to suffer for others.

When I consider the comprehensive care of *Jehovah Jireh* ("The Lord will provide") in my own experience, my mind immediately turns to the most concentrated exposure to God's gracious provision my wife and I have ever experienced.

One unforgettable year Maureen and I ventured on a faith journey, ministering in a dozen Asian countries. Everywhere we went, God met our needs in unmistakable ways. I vividly recall entering China during the first week of January with clothing suited to the tropical Philippines. At our first hotel, two winter parkas in our sizes were in our room! We asked about these at the front desk and they motioned for us to keep whatever the previous guests had left. We had come to give to the church, and God seemed to be saying, "Let me take care of you."

Arriving in Japan later that spring with enough money for no more than a week, we expected to make two brief stops and fly home. But God had other plans. For the next two months we helped with a church plant in Osaka and evangelized

---

a. Eph. 5:25

freely in English classes day and night. Preparing to leave, we turned in our pay stubs for cash and found that God had provided the exact amount of money we had spent for the whole year's travel! He "picked up the tab" right before our eyes. We think of that year in the terms Nehemiah used of the Israelites' wilderness sojourn, "They lacked nothing, their clothes did not wear out, nor did their feet become swollen."[a]

When we returned to the United States, an ideal ministry awaited us. As directors of a residence for international students, we had the chance to share Christ's love with those who would likely never enter a Christian family's home. We hosted twenty-five residents with space for travelers. We fed them, took them on trips, and helped them navigate life in a foreign country. And, in both casual and planned venues, we shared the gospel. Maureen and I transitioned from being taken care of to taking care of others.

As our journey in the days ahead takes us to various provision topics, let's consider the ways we have been cared for as well as the people God has asked us to care for. I love how Paul puts it: "Praise be to the God and Father of our LORD Jesus Christ, the Father of compassion and the God of all comfort, *who comforts us* in all our troubles, *so that we can comfort* those in any trouble with the comfort we ourselves have received from God."[b]

He is the standard and the motivation for a life of caring service.

a. Neh. 9:21 b. 2 Cor. 1:3-4

He chose David from tending the sheep
to be the shepherd of his people.

—Psalm 78:70–71

Called to Care

Ω Pastor Jamie and I met in Israel during the year I was interviewing Bedouin shepherds and studying pastoralism.[1] Though the ultimate purpose of my research was to reconsider what the Bible says to *spiritual* shepherds, I hadn't planned on interviewing pastors as a part of my field research. In an informal get-together, when I least expected it, Jamie's story convinced me afresh that God fully intends to use the shepherd image to shape the identity of his ministers.[2]

Back in 1996 Jamie wasn't looking to change careers, nor was he expecting God to speak to him in some mysterious way. He was happy with his family, his church life, and his job in Southern England. While walking home one day, he looked across a riverbank at a lush green field where a shepherd tended his flock. As he stopped to reflect on the scene, a sheep came trotting in his direction. Jamie began to realize that the sheep was headed for the riverbank. He began to motion with his hands to alert the shepherd, but he was too far away. Jamie then began to shout at the sheep to discourage it from coming any further. But the ewe lumbered to the edge of the embankment and, without hesitation, stumbled down the hill into the murky river.

With a thick coat of wool now weighed down in water and mud, the animal began to struggle. Helplessly stuck, her slick hooves felt in vain for a solid bottom. Smitten with sympathy, Jamie pried off his shoes and hustled down the embankment into the river. Knee-deep in muck, he too began to struggle. But seeing the sheep's pathetic predicament, he persisted in wading across to help. With no small effort he hauled the animal out and scrambled up the precipitous embankment.

As the young English businessman stumbled across the field that afternoon, soggy ewe atop his shoulders, he heard an inaudible voice inside his heart say, "Jamie, this is my plan for your life: to rescue my lost sheep, one at a time." The message was that simple and that direct. And that moment changed the course of his life.

Following his "calling," Jamie cautiously launched a ministry now operating in several cities in the United Kingdom and Australia. Their mission is simply to minister to anyone they find "lost," one at a time. They offer counseling, housing, food, job training, and friendship. Shepherding requires a wide range of competencies and tasks, all of which begin with a compassionate heart for individual sheep.

It was only natural for God to call shepherds to be leaders of his community. David, like Abraham and Moses, was a herder before he was summoned to spiritual shepherding. "He *chose* David his servant and took him from the sheep pens; from tending the sheep he brought him to be the shepherd of his people Jacob, of Israel his inheritance. And David shepherded them with integrity of heart; with skillful hands he led them."[a]

David's dramatic calling as a young man left an unforgettable memory that would brace him in days of doubt ahead.[b] But the pages of Scripture are filled with stories of lesser known figures who simply responded to a more general invitation to serve God's people. They too became God's undershepherds.

When Jesus called a group of unremarkable individuals to serve with him, he sent them out as spiritual shepherds to "the lost sheep of Israel."[c] This mission defined their ministry *as an extension of his pastoral service* to those who were sick and in bondage. Their work was a reflection of the concerns of the Good Shepherd who gave his life for the flock.[d] Every disciple was a shepherd called to the messy work of caring for people, of shouldering their various needs, and bearing them for Christ, the Chief Shepherd.[e]

At the beginning of this season of reflection, let's remember our call to our particular ministry. Not everyone is called as dramatically as Pastor Jamie. Not everyone is called to vocational ministry. But something in his story reminds us all of what we are each summoned to do. To get dirty helping the people Jesus came to recover. Can we recall an occasion when a specific personal mission was planted in our hearts? Did an undeniable sense of unique destiny in the Kingdom of God surface during a particular season in life? This spiritual calling, this destiny, this identity is more transcendent than a job description. It is our life's mission.

---

a. Ps. 78:70–72 (cf. Amos 7:14) b. 1 Sam. 16 c. Matt. 10:6 d. John 10:11 e. 1 Pet. 5:4

Let's reconnect with our individual "riverbank" experience before we go any further.

For those of us who have been in the fields for a long time, we may be aware of major adjustments to our calling through the years. The original vision didn't turn out to be the detailed blueprint we assumed, and some of the changes have taken us by surprise. How has shepherding changed in each new setting? In our reassignments, what core elements of the original call have remained intact?

Finally, consider how God has shepherded us during these changes. Occasionally *we've* been the soggy ewe atop *his* shoulders. Can we learn something from the way he calls...and re-calls?

Unfortunately, while many of us did experience a strong sense of calling earlier in our lives, we have grown "weary in well-doing."[a] Perhaps the culture's view of our work has dented our self-image, prompting us to long for a "real job." Leadership is often thankless, with more criticism and opposition than we ever dreamed of. Every day, disillusioned ministers walk away from a calling they once cherished, but now doubt.

---

a. Gal. 6:9

Parents disappear from homes with children they once had a vision to disciple. Caregivers of all types give up caring.

May God use this season of reflection to inspire us afresh with renewed vigor to serve his flock, whatever that flock happens to be.

*Water will gush forth in the wilderness
and streams in the desert.*

—Isaiah 35:6

Streams in the Desert

The deserts and wildernesses of the Middle East only grudgingly provide their most precious commodity. The clouds seem to forget their annual assignment to convey water to a parched landscape. Many plants survive years without rain by stealing moisture from dew that lingers in the rocky soil. The Jericho rose is famous for its ability to exist, literally, for centuries without a drop of moisture.

But humans and flock animals are not designed to survive drought. The dread of it never subsides. Years without rain bring devastating losses, especially among the pregnant or nursing ewes and their young. An eight-year drought choked the Arabian Peninsula during the 1950s and 1960s. Thousands of animals perished. Without better grazing somewhere, shepherds helplessly stare at flocks dying of dehydration, lifeless lumps of wool littering the desert floor. Their livelihood evaporates in the desert sun before their eyes.

Languishing in penetrating heat, shepherds prayerfully pine for rain. The poet Ad-Dindan expresses the rain-obsession of desert Arabs in his petition for an early winter storm:

From You I ask a night stretching from the east towards
    al-Kharrah
Heralded by flashes of lightning and rolling thunder as
    unmistakable signs
A night covered as if with an encampment of white tents
And crisscrossed by cloud racks chasing one another
    like playful she-camels with young.
The raincloud's arrival cheers the worn-out, skinny animals
And brings forth the plant life from the empty,
    barren gravel plains[1]

Imagine the anguish when lightning flashes and thunder rolls, but rain refuses to follow. A whole winter can pass that way.

When the sky does empty life-giving buckets of water, the challenge is to manage access to it. A cloudburst miles away may create a river in a nearby *wadi* (valley), only to leave a desiccated landscape again within hours. Ironically, desert dwellers fear a flash flood in these non-absorbent places almost as much as drought.[2] In the Sinai every sizeable downpour results in wadi floods.[3] Though the psalmist's "throat is parched" in a wilderness setting, he prays, "Save me, O God, for the *waters* have come up to my neck. I sink in the *miry depths*, where there is no foothold. I have come into the *deep waters*; the *floods* engulf me."[a] A herder yearning for rain may find himself helplessly watching his drowning flock wash away with his answered prayers. Desert Arabs say, "In three things have no trust: a slave, a rutting camel, and a *flood*."[4]

What a shepherd really desires are the *still* waters that follow the rains. Sheep can safely satisfy themselves by the puddles and pools left once the floods have passed. Shepherds prepare for these bursts of water by creating dams and channels leading to temporary reservoirs.

---

a. Ps. 69:1-3

With images of a renewed wilderness, Isaiah stirred generations to long for the Messianic Era: "Water will gush forth in the wilderness and streams in the desert. The burning sand will become a pool, the thirsty ground bubbling springs."[a] Spiritual droughts and desert dangers would give way to wilderness

blossoms and bubbling springs of national wellbeing. A renewing downpour of God's grace would revive an exiled people in their spiritual famine.

Unfortunately, the community the prophets addressed were too easily satisfied with substitutes. "My people have committed two sins: They have forsaken me, the spring of living water, and have dug their own cisterns, broken cisterns that cannot hold water."[b] In biblical times fresh, running, "living" water was preferred over stagnant cistern water. Centuries would pass before the "spring" arrived in person.

The Messiah came offering living water that could quench a soul's thirst—"a spring of water welling up to eternal life."[c] Jesus audaciously promised that the empty and parched person could become a reservoir of refreshment for others: "If anyone is thirsty, let him come to me and drink. Whoever believes in me, as the Scripture has said, streams of living water will flow from within him."[d] Perhaps he

a. Isa. 35:6-7 b. Jer. 2:13 c. John 4:14 d. John 7:37-38

had in mind the proverb, "The words of a man's mouth are deep waters, but the fountain of wisdom is a bubbling brook."[a] Jesus was leading them to "the fountain of Israel" where, in the words of the psalmist, "The channels of God are always full of water."[b] The most vivid expression of the revivifying power of living water is Ezekiel's vision of the river of God restoring even the Dead Sea back to life.[c]

In a surreal heavenly scene recorded in Revelation, the Divine Shepherd perpetually quenches the thirst of all who worship him:

> They are before the throne of God and serve him day and night in his temple; and he who sits on the throne will spread his tent over them. Never again will they hunger; never again will they thirst. The sun will not beat upon them, nor any scorching heat. For the Lamb at the center of the throne will be their shepherd; he will lead them to springs of living water. And God will wipe away every tear from their eyes. (Rev. 7:15–17)

Let's consider for a moment our own parched souls. The psalmist expresses a spiritual yearning: "My soul thirsts for you in a dry and weary land where there is no water."[d] How long has it been since we tasted fresh life-giving water? Maybe we've dehydrated in the sun while providing pools of refreshment for others. Where are the still waters for us? *Our own quenched thirst is the most sustaining source of strength for serving others.* "Above all else, guard your heart, for it is the wellspring of life."[e]

What about our flocks? Are they sipping regularly from still, sweet streams or are they gasping helplessly in the heat? Have we channeled water into protected reservoirs for relaxed drinking?

---

a. Prov. 18:4 b. Ps. 68:26; Ps. 65:9 (author's translation) c. Ezek. 47 d. Ps. 63:1 e. Prov. 4:23

Do we inspire a longing for spiritual oases in our ministries?

I wonder if our flocks feel summoned to still waters or thrust into rushing turbulence.

Let's begin to think honestly and constructively about reviving and refreshing the people who work with us. Every Christian organization, church, or family can be a reservoir of renewal—a place where the Shepherd of Heaven is allowed to deliver on his promise of streams in the desert.

Spring up, O well!
Sing about the well that the princes dug.

—Numbers 21:17–18

Spring Up, O Well!

𝔑 I became especially interested in desert wells in the Sinai when my son and I met Salima who, with a handful of coworkers, dug a thirty-foot well in a valley with nothing but hand trowels! My curiosity piqued, I pushed questions at him through the translator: "How did you know where to dig? Did you have any doubts at ten feet? At twenty?"

To the first question Salima pointed to the vegetation nearby. The particular plants growing there were signals for water under the surface of the *wadi's* gravelly floor. He then pointed to the *wadi* walls. Though first all we saw was monotonous "wilderness brown," we did eventually make out the dark line of non-porous shale zigzagging down the *wadi* walls, pointing toward the spot where they dug. Obviously, knowledge and perseverance are requirements for survival in this part of the world. I've since learned that some wells in the desert may be seventy feet deep or more.

Pastoralists are ingenious when it comes to finding, keeping, maintaining, and guarding their water sources. They make use of natural cisterns and construct their own dams, cisterns, wells, and connected "well-chains" that feed into each other.[1] Nineteenth-century German explorer Alois Musil listed forty-five Arabic names for different types of natural, enhanced, or wholly artificial water-retaining structures.[2] Incredibly, crude cisterns can store water from a desert flood for up to two years.[3] Bedouin cover them with heavy stones to avoid evaporation, contamination, and water theft. The stone lids also keep thirsty animals from pushing each other into a water pit. I have even heard of children who've been shoved into wells by a thirsty flock.

Water is rarely accessible without knowledge and hard work. The most treasured source of water is the oasis, with underground springs that nurture a thriving tropical garden in the midst of a barren wasteland. But even these springs can be contaminated.[4] For skilled shepherds, other means exist to find water trapped by nature. Sometimes they locate water that has traveled through porous rock and collected in hidden pools. However, the most common way to get at underground water is the hardest way. Dig wells. The deserts of Saudia Arabia today are peppered with over seven hundred *makhafir* (manmade pools) that hold from one hundred thousand to one million gallons of water.[5]

Tales of conflicts over wells abound in Arab lore. One author claims it is the third favorite theme in Bedouin folk tales (next to thieves and raiding).[6] Well stories feature in the patriarchal narratives of the Bible too, some near Beer-Sheva—literally, "Well of Oath."[7] You can imagine Isaac's delight over the words of his servants, "We've found water!"[a] But Isaac's reopening of Abraham's wells elicited an attack by the

___
a. Gen. 26:32

local herders of Gerar. After digging new wells, these too were contested with the claim, "The water is ours!"^a

While disputes over water sources are constant, a widespread Bedouin tradition allows passing herdsmen to stop and water their flocks at a private well. But *only* once. This custom reflects a tacit admission that one day these same owners may find themselves in need of another's hospitality. I think the proverb, "Make a friend before you need one," explains a good bit of this kind of desert generosity. Theologically, however, the custom reflects a recognition that everything we have ultimately comes from God.

As we trekked in the Sinai, I couldn't help but think about a man in the Bible who found water in these mountains. About thirty-five hundred years ago, seven daughters of Jethro, a Midianite priest, came to water their flocks at a well near Mt. Sinai only to find abusive herdsmen intent on driving them away. To their surprise an Egyptian came to their rescue and then watered their flocks.[8] This gesture initiated a long relationship between Moses, former prince of Egypt, and the family of Jethro. It also launched Moses' forty-year career as a shepherd in the deserts surrounding Sinai. Like any new shepherd, Moses would learn how to keep a flock alive and thriving in this harsh environment. His training would necessarily have involved learning the secret sources of water.

God later launched Moses into another forty-year career as a spiritual shepherd for a nation. Much of his experience among Jethro's flocks surely helped shape his understanding of leadership. However, shepherding know-how also got him into trouble.

---

a. Gen. 26:20

In Exodus 17 Moses was commanded to strike a rock at Horeb (another name for Sinai) to provide water for God's thirsty people. Because the mountains of the Sinai Peninsula are made of non-porous granite, Moses could only trust God for a miracle. When water gushed from the rock everyone knew it was a divine wonder.[9] Including Moses.

A similar story in Numbers 20 is often confused with this one. Asked this time to *speak* to a rock, Moses instead strikes it, incurring God's judgment on himself. An instant flood satisfied the parched crowd, but the veteran leader of Israel would not be allowed into the Promised Land.

Most of us shudder at the harsh judgment for Moses. After all, hadn't God ordered him to strike a rock once before? Yes, but in this second case, they were north of the Sinai Peninsula in the Wilderness of Zin, where the rock is a porous type of limestone (marl). Here water collects in hidden pools, leaks along natural seams, and drains out the walls. Moses scolded the people with a rhetorical question, "Listen you rebels. Must *we* bring water out of this rock?!"[a] Angrily, Moses rapped the limestone with his staff twice, presumably where the knowledgeable shepherd recognized the evidence of previous seepage. He probably broke open a calcified

a. Num. 20:10

plug that had formed over one of nature's faucets. Instead of a miracle, Moses used an old shepherd's trick, and God was not honored as the source of water. For this reason he was judged: "Because you did not trust in me enough to honor me as holy in the sight of the Israelites, you will not bring this community into the land I give them."[a]

Well-digging has personal implications. I became reacquainted with a childhood friend whose faith was floundering. In his words, "I stopped reading my Bible because I got nothing out of it. Prayer got me nowhere. In church I was just going through the motions." Over the course of the ensuing conversation I suggested that years of Christian school and church had created a bigger spiritual challenge for us than for those without any foundation. It seems that we need to pray, read, and reflect more, not less, because these actions can so easily become meaningless and rote rituals. We have to keep digging because we know where the water is. It's just sometimes deeper than we wish.

Well-digging stories remind us that a shepherd's knowledge, skill, and perseverance are critically necessary to access resources for our flocks. Leading means knowing where and how to dig. But, like rain, every life-sustaining necessity ultimately falls from heaven. The question left for us is, "Do we direct the attention of those we serve to the Source or do we sometimes, in exasperation, use the 'tricks' of skills and strategies to accomplish heaven's work?" Paul resisted these urges, clinging nakedly to divine promise, "so that your faith might not rest on men's wisdom, but on God's power."[b] *Leading means trusting.*

---

a. Num. 20:12 b. 1 Cor. 2:5

I will restore Israel to its pasture
and its hunger shall be satisfied.

—Jeremiah 50:19

DAY 6

Greener Pastures

ℒ After a day of field interviews, my translator Muaz took my son and me back to his house for a welcome dish of rice and chicken. I asked if his elderly, widowed grandmother living nearby might answer some questions about traditional shepherding life. Muaz said she'd be happy to. After dinner we walked to Uma-Nabila's little cement house and there I met a woman weathered by a century of life in the sun. I was quite anxious to get a female perspective on herding and to catch a glimpse of life in the early twentieth century.

What surprised me most in the conversation was how casually Uma-Nabila referred to travelling when she was a young girl, ninety years ago. Her family lived in tents and caves in what is today Jordan, moving where the grasses were good and a deal could be struck for pasture land. They respected the ancient *Hima* system which protects common fields from overgrazing.[1] Some pastures nearby might have been suitable for grazing in the short run but kept off limits by the tribal leaders for long-term stability.

I asked Uma-Nabila how far her family roamed back before the current national boundaries were set. She said they moved all over, and that for several years they lived near Hebron. This ancient village, known to the Bible's patriarchal

herders, is on the west side of the Dead Sea, in a completely different region.[2] I met other shepherds in my travels who drifted from Saudi Arabia all the way to Syria. I have since discovered that, driven by the prospect of famine, herding tribes may travel fifteen hundred miles annually with one goal in mind: greener pastures.

When pastures flourish somewhere else, the news spreads quickly to desperate shepherds.[3] A poet-scout runs with the message, "Follow me to rain-fed lands as yet untouched by any creature except the lark who fills the air with his tunes while he dives and turns above an earth that burst into flower."[4] A shepherd poet who knows the harshness of death-dealing drought sings about the prospect of a rain storm's seed-producing capacity:

> Valleys drenched by decree of the Almighty at once spring to life
> Along with the precipitation, God sends down the fresh
> annuals' seeds
> The land, before a barren waste, attired itself in green sprouts
> And burst into blossom after God had washed away its crust
> of dirt.[5]

The notion of gods and kings providing their subjects with green pastures was widespread in the ancient world. A common refrain in royal hymns was the petition, "May the people lie down in grassy pastures under your reign, [enjoying] abundance."[6] On the ascension of a famous Akkadian ruler, "All the lands were lying down in grassy pastures, their people experienced happiness. Their king, the shepherd Naram-Sin, rose like the sun on the holy throne."[7]

I only recently discovered that the name "Eden" comes from an Akkadian word referring to verdant wilderness.[8] A desert bursting with green grasses is the paradise for which every shepherd longs, a glimpse of the primal paradise of Genesis 1 and 2. In this lively landscape the psalmist sees herds and plants singing praise to their Creator: "The meadows are covered with flocks, and the valleys are mantled with grain; they shout for joy and sing."[a]

Psalm 23 mentions green pastures and a "table" prepared in the wilderness setting. Perhaps the author has in mind the flat desert tablelands surrounded by hills where prowling predators await. The Israelites had doubted that God could provide for them in their desert sojourn, asking, "Can God spread a table in the wilderness?"[b] The psalmist knows of a Divine Shepherd who can and will. Psalm 23 ends with an image of the sheep's permanent residence in the house of its host.

The psalmist was likely longing for Mount Zion, God's holy dwelling situated at the heart of the Promised Land. The countryside of Canaan was the "holy pasture" to which God was guiding his newly liberated people.[c] This "land flowing with milk and honey" was a paradise for shepherds and farmers. Milk comes from livestock, and honey—either from the date palm or from bee hives—symbolized nature's accessible bounty. Jerusalem would become the center of this holy pasture, the place of God's pastoral dwelling.

---

a. Ps. 65:13 b. Ps. 78:19 c. Exod. 15:13

Israel was meant to learn that they could trust God to lead them to green pastures to satisfy their hunger. A deeper lesson to learn, ironically, was discerned by their adversaries first: "Whoever found them devoured them; their enemies said, 'We are not guilty, for they sinned against *the LORD, their true pasture*, the LORD, the hope of their fathers.'"[a] God is not only the source of the basic necessities of life; God *is* life.

Early in our journey in the wilderness, let's consider the ways God has prepared a table for us in the wilderness. Recount occasions when he has provided unexpectedly and supernaturally in desert-like places. Which seasons of life and ministry were as dry as a desert drought? Has God led us out of our helplessness and hopelessness to greener pastures? I can remember vividly occasions when God provided dramatically for our family after a period of waiting and wondering. In other areas of life and ministry I find myself still hoping for a breakthrough, for greener pastures.

a. Jer. 50:7

Let's go deeper and consider the difference between seeing God as the giver of things that sustain life and understanding God as life itself. Jesus came to *give* life, but he also said *"I am the life."*[b] Have we forsaken our true pasture? Perhaps the longing for "greener pastures" in our ministry setting may be the result of missing the Provision right before our eyes. *Has God brought us into a wilderness to teach us that only God can satisfy our deepest longings?*

Finally, reflect with me on leadership as thoughtful hospitality. I recall fondly the years we hosted students and scholars from across the globe in The International Fellowship House. Maureen learned how to cook Asian, African, and Latin American foods so that we could treat our guests to sumptuous banquets suited to their appetites. Our table provided a taste of God's provision to those surrounded by a desert of enigmatic Western ways that heightened their feelings of separation and loneliness. They could safely recline in green pastures. Our mission was to help them see in this provision the gracious Provider.

b. John 10:10; 11:25; 14:6

Do you love me?
Feed my sheep.

—John 21:17

Feed My Sheep

One thing I learned during my experience out on the range was that if you care for sheep, you feed them *all the time*. I was surprised when we moved three or four times throughout the day to make sure that the flocks got the right mix and variety. The obvious concern was providing the flocks with adequate, balanced nutrition. When we came in at dusk, their grazing intake was supplemented again, this time with a meal of enriched grain. Feeding is the only way to secure healthy production. Without it, there is less milk and fiber, and fewer healthy births.

But of course, *proper* feeding is the issue. The animals get into poisonous plants, eat weeds that provide only empty calories, and kill themselves eating trash. I couldn't tell the difference between one form of vegetation and another, but soon discovered that shepherds have a sophisticated knowledge about their animals' consumption. Every region has its own combination of soil, climate, land formation and plant communities. Each is a "mosaic of micro-environments" that the shepherd must master.[1]

An early twentieth century researcher found that Bedouin tribes in the Sinai knew the attributes of over one hundred plants.[2] They knew which were good for sheep and which for goats; which were seasonal and which perennial; which were medicinal, and for what ailments and which animals; and which were vulnerable to overgrazing. Another writer describes 271 plants and shrubs that grow across all the Arab desert lands. Clearly, if you care for sheep, you need to know what your flock is eating. Empty calories just won't do.

In a touching rabbinic *midrash* (explanation) on Psalm 78, God watches David lead his flocks out to feed. According to this imaginative commentary, David's royal calling was based on his care and skill with his animals *during feeding*.

> He would prevent the adult sheep from heading first to the pasture lands. He would lead the younger sheep out first so that they would graze off the soft, juicy grass. Then he would take the older sheep to graze off the medium grade grass; finally he would take the young robust sheep and let them graze off the tough graded grass. The Holy One said: Let he who knows how to shepherd sheep according to their needs come and shepherd my people.[3]

In a memorable passage in John 21:15-23, Jesus questions Peter's love for him. Three times he asks, "Do you *love* me?" Three times Peter answers definitively, "Yes, you *know* that I do." Each time the Lord follows with a challenge to "*feed* my sheep." There are several semantic subtleties in this interchange. Jesus uses two different words for loving, and Peter uses two different words for knowing. The disciple who denied Jesus is obviously distressed by the probing repetition of the questions and wants to convey the certainty of his love.

Jesus apparently doesn't want confessions of sentiment alone. He wants love expressed in action described by another pair of synonyms. He uses *poimaino*, the general term for shepherding, once. But in the first and last command he employs the verb *bosko*, a herding term that refers specifically to feeding. The Lord was emphasizing to Peter that *leading means feeding*.

Peter would have understood the significance of the imagery from his Bible. The Shepherd of Israel had provided richly satisfying "heavenly bread" in

the wilderness centuries earlier.[a] While manna was a miraculous means of physical sustenance, the "bread of angels" was more importantly an image of divine revelation.[b] The people of God were ultimately sustained by *the word of God*.[c] Jesus was

calling Peter to express his love for him by providing *spiritual* food.

The connection between caring for people as sheep and nourishing them with God's word is plainly visible in the story of the feeding of the five thousand: "When Jesus landed and saw a large crowd, he had *compassion* on them, because they were *like sheep* without a shepherd. *So he began teaching them many things.*"[d]

a. Ps. 78:24-29 b. Ps. 78:25 c. Deut. 8:3 d. Mark 6:34

Like the Divine Shepherd in the Old Testament, Jesus cared for a hungry crowd by giving them physical food, *and* he reached out to a greater hunger with God's life-giving words. In fact, Jesus turned every crisis into a teaching moment.

Paul said, "Let no one deceive you with empty words."[a] He understood the need for "healthy teaching," encouraging constant nourishment on God's words.[4] Paul believed that scriptural truth alone is sufficient for rebuking, correcting and training in righteousness,[b] and that these forms of feeding were pastoral tasks. The apocryphal book Sirach had earlier used the same terms for God who, "rebukes and trains and teaches them, and turns them back, as a shepherd his flock."[c]

It was twenty years ago that my wife Maureen and I spent a memorable winter in China meeting with members of the underground church. We carried in our backpacks Christian books and tapes that would be useful as a portable seminary. Chinese Bibles took up the most space. When we met our first contact, she informed us that we would need to speak in coded language: "Just refer to what you brought as 'bread.'" That night we served "bread" to a hungry pastor who had traveled for days from a remote province where his whole church had just been jailed. He was hoping for "bread" to take back to his discouraged flock. The unforgettable look of gratitude on his face reminds me that this world's only source of life and hope is God's word.

Will you join me for some honest self-assessment? What do *we* as leaders eat? To what sources do we return for our soul's primary sustenance? Is our "diet" rich in God's word? Are we as leaders good readers? Do we really *study* scripture and *meditate* on it daily, relishing its insights as spiritual delicacies? Do we supplement this feeling with devotional classics, theological treasures, and inspiring

---

a. Eph. 5:6 b. 2 Tim. 3:16 (author's translation); 1 Tim. 4:6 (NASB) c. Sirach 18:13 (NRSV)

biographies? Or do we fill our hungry void with the empty calories provided on television and by endless "browsing" on the internet?

If leadership is a form of hospitality, and teaching is the highest expression of that hospitality, then we should ask some pointed questions about our teaching leadership—whether it be in preaching, counseling, or other kinds of teaching venues. What do we feed those we serve? Are they getting frequent meals rich in nutrition, or is it old and trivial stuff? Would Paul criticize us for empty words? As a teacher my favorite compliment is, "Thank you for feeding my soul."

Perhaps we do feed our people well, but *do not teach them how to feed themselves*. We ignore their habits of browsing on sickening trash, and the vacuous options and synthetic substitutes that our culture puts under their noses. There is a famine of God's word in our time. There are "great crowds with nothing to eat."[a] If we "send them away hungry, they may collapse on the way."[b] Let's nourish God's flock back to health with the transforming words of life. And insist on some discriminating browsing.

a. Mark 8:1 b. Matt. 15:32

Know well the condition of your flocks,
and pay attention to your herds.

—Proverbs 27:23

The Shepherd Healer

I'm in awe that the health and well-being of hundreds of animals is often left in the hands of a single person out in the wilderness. The vast variety of ills and harmful habits that befall sheep around the world is almost comical, except when you consider that a household's livelihood is completely at risk every day. An account from Wales could as easily have come from ancient Palestine:

> My mother, a hill farmer of consummate skill, is still amazed at the variety of ways a sheep can find to die. Even the hardy Welsh mountain breed with which I was brought up are susceptible to braxy, pulpy kidney, staggers, pneumonia, pasturella, twin lamb disease, cancer, hypothermia in the winter, maggots in the summer, scab, scrapie, foxes, crows, and dogs. They push their heads through fences and get stuck. They climb trees to pick at foliage and get hung up by their horns or legs. They fall down banks, get bitten by snakes and stung by wasps. They tumble into ponds and streams. They gorge themselves on fallen ash leaves, roll on their backs and blow up like balloons. They poison themselves on ragwort. Rams' horns regularly grow into their own heads...They starve, freeze, get depressed and fall ill—but a good shepherd can counter every affliction.[1]

But a good shepherd can counter every affliction.

What an amazing affirmation after such a litany of threats. Now imagine facing this host of diseases and risks in hostile desert environments without the benefit of modern vaccinations and medications. Alone. With just a small first aid pouch and an oral tradition of natural remedies.

Contagious diseases such as footrot, sore mouth, lockjaw, and pneumonia present the greatest health risks. "A scabby goat will infect the whole herd," says an Arab proverb.[2] Good shepherds have to be constantly alert for animals that become lame or listless or who exhibit lumps, lesions, sores, or swelling. They need to check eyes, ears, mouths, noses, and hoofs...monitor weight loss...examine feces. They must recognize the earliest symptoms of a variety of diseases, especially those that can spread through a flock within hours. Otherwise they'll watch helplessly as their treasured assets collapse. One young shepherd confessed his sense of complicity after a lethal epidemic: "We lost a lot of ewes. It was discouraging. We thought we were killing them."[3] Only an attentive and knowledgeable shepherd is competent to *counter every affliction.*

In his classic, *A Shepherd Looks at Psalm 23*, Philip Keller describes the anxiety and danger caused by parasites, just one of the many sources of disease:

> For relief from this agonizing annoyance sheep will deliberately beat their heads against the trees, rocks, posts, or brush. They will rub them in the soil and thrash around against woody growth. In extreme cases of infestation a sheep may even kill itself in a frenzied endeavor to gain respite from the aggravation. Often advanced stages of infection from these flies will lead to blindness. Because of this, when the nose flies hover around the neck, some of the sheep become frantic with fear and panic in their attempt to escape their tormentors. They will stamp their feet erratically and race from place to place.[4]

One ancient remedy for parasitic tormentors was olive oil. Rubbing it around the nose and eyes of an animal would create a protective coating. The ancient's aspirin, oil, was used as a general salve for most injuries. Traditional Middle Eastern pastoralists have made skilled use of certain plants and natural products with medicinal qualities.

They still boil *nytùn* for eye and skin problems and *makhrùt* and *makhatab* roots to wash infected wounds. Salt's healing properties are exploited. Pitch, sulphur, or urine supply an alkaline wash. Wine and vinegar serve as antiseptics.

What strikes me in all of these procedures is that *shepherding requires touch*. It might be running their hands along the spine, lifting the eyelids, or pulling back the ears. It might be rubbing oil or applying a poultice. Whatever the condition, shepherds can't simply stand at a distance. They need to touch the sheep. Each night the sheep must "pass under the shepherd's rod"[a] to be checked individually for signs of illness, wounds, or weight loss. Such preventative, precautionary, proactive measures only happen with direct physical contact.

The Good Shepherd made compassionate healing a central feature of his ministry. "Jesus went through all the towns and villages, teaching in their synagogues, preaching the good news of the kingdom, and healing every disease and sickness.

---

a. Ezek. 20:37

When he saw the crowds, he had compassion on them, because they were harassed and helpless, like sheep without a shepherd."[a] This ministry of healing was predicted in the Old Testament, when God speaks of Israel in exile: "Nevertheless, I will bring *health* and *healing* to [Jerusalem]; I will *heal* my people and will let them enjoy abundant peace and security."[b] God had promised to rescue a wounded flock, poorly served by shepherds who had not "strengthened the weak or healed the sick or bound up the injured."[c] They hadn't understood that *leading means healing*.

What catches my attention is that while Jesus often healed simply by speaking a word, in many cases he chose to heal with his hands. With compassion he reached out and touched an "untouchable" with leprosy.[d] With compassion he touched the eyes of two blind men[e] and, after applying spit-mud, laid his healing hands on another.[f] He put his fingers in a deaf man's ears and then touched his tongue.[g] Even during his arrest the Lord graciously healed the ear of the high priest's servant with a touch.[h]

Jesus' compassion for the crowds was like that of a shepherd viewing a poorly managed flock. He asked his disciples to entreat God for help. Having shared his vision and his burden, he then sent *them* out "to the lost sheep of Israel" with a ministry of word and touch: "As you go, preach this message: 'The kingdom of heaven is near.' Heal the sick, raise the dead, cleanse those who have leprosy, drive out demons."[i] The disciples became extensions of the Lord's healing ministry to both body and soul.

The expectation upon God's undershepherds is still to strengthen the weak, heal the sick, bind up the injured, and liberate the possessed. I wonder if our ministry environments fully include those with disabilities. Do we welcome those

a. Matt. 9:35–36 cf. Isa. 57:18–19; Hosea 6:1 b. Jer. 33:6 c. Ezek. 34:4 d. Mark 1:41 e. Matt. 20:34 f. Mark 8:23 g. Mark 7:33 h. Luke 22:51 i. Matt. 10:6-8

silently enduring the shame and suffering of AIDS? Do we promote deliverance ministry? Do we take health for granted?

Do we recognize the subtle symptoms of our flocks' ailments in a toxic social environment, saturated with sensual stimulation? Have we created a safe place for fragile souls who are suffering emotionally, overwhelmed with grief or chronic depression? Do we afford the time necessary to care for those fighting long-term and terminal illness? Are those who are suffering the most, touched the most?

Veterinarians look for the basic illnesses common to a flock. I wonder if we might learn the value of constantly assessing the presence of the "seven deadly sins"—lust, gluttony, greed, sloth, anger, envy, and pride. Is there some way to quarantine (remove from positions of influence) those who are contagious? Does any disease spread more quickly than slander? The health issues of a single member are health issues for a whole flock. We should be ready to *counter every affliction.*

Sometimes sin is the source of physical sickness. The apostle James advises his congregations to pursue this possibility:

> Is any one of you sick? He should call the elders of the church to pray over him and anoint him with oil in the name of the LORD. And the prayer offered in faith will make the sick person well; the LORD will raise him up. If he has sinned, he will be forgiven. Therefore confess your sins to each other and pray for each other so that you may be healed. The prayer of a righteous man is powerful and effective. (James 5:14–16)

To counter every affliction we need a shepherd's "pouch" with emergency items: oil for prayer, Scripture for encouragement, phone numbers for crisis assistance. More fundamentally, we need the compassionate disposition of the Great Physician who would stop a crowd to touch a wounded soul.

He will gather the lambs in his arms, and carry them
in his bosom, and gently lead the nursing ewes.

—Isaiah 40:11

Midwives and Nurses

I remember the first time I saw a group of newborn lambs. They were in a small cave-like pen in Bethlehem in 1986. Small and fragile, they wobbled in the dimly lit enclosure, directed by the owner's family to their mothers for the first feeding.

They say that lambing season is the "crisis of the shepherds' year"—the true test of their commitment, stamina, and skill.[1] What happens in the critical moments around birth initiates the uniquely intimate relationship between shepherd and sheep. Successful births often require human intervention. As midwives, shepherds are engaged quite physically, reaching inside the ewes and carefully repositioning the lambs so that the head and front legs come out first. Some lambs are too big to be born easily. Some are too small to live long. Sometimes the mother does not naturally lick the membrane off the newborn. Often she doesn't nurse well. Every shepherd wants each newborn to live.

You have to fight for some to make it.

That night in Bethlehem the ewes had given birth without serious complications and all the newborns were happily nursing. Bonding had begun between ewe and lamb and between shepherd and sheep. The next critical moment in these emotional relationships would be weaning. A ewe and her lamb may "cry" for days and remember each other for months.[2] The shepherd is by then intimately attached to both, gently caring for each in their separation.

A Syrian shepherd describes typical births on the open range and the shepherd's automatic response:

> Sometimes the ewes will give birth to lambs while he is on the mountains. He places these young lambs, or those of them that have broken legs, right inside his coat. Every now and then he will be seen gathering the tenderest grass to feed them. It is both amusing and pathetic to see these lambs raising their heads and bleating, while the mothers are following his tracks.[3]

 Care for mothers and their young requires a remarkable blend of skill and gentleness that surfaces during the night of birth. Jacob had been a gentle shepherd. When he and Esau were reconciled after years of estrangement, Jacob still insisted on traveling at the pace of his needy ewes: "My LORD knows that the children are tender and that I must care for the ewes and cows that are nursing their young. If they are driven hard just one day, all the animals will die."[a]

Skill and concern for nursing mothers and their young was apparently important in God's choice of David to lead his people. "He also chose David his servant and took him from the sheepfolds; *from the care of the ewes with suckling lambs*[4] he brought him to shepherd Jacob his

a. Gen. 33:13

people, and Israel his inheritance. So he shepherded them according to the integrity of his heart, and guided them with his *skillful hands*."[a] God chose a man who had been intimately involved in preserving and nurturing fragile new life to take care of a people God himself had gently led in the wilderness.[5]

Unfortunately, there came a time when David allowed the privileges and perquisites of his position to cloud his pastoral mission. He used his royal power to take advantage of loyal servants. I'm referring to the affair with Bathsheba and the "murder" of Uriah. To expose the nature of the crime, Nathan told him a gut-wrenching parable about a poor man and his pet lamb. "He raised it, and it grew up with him and his children. It shared his food, drank from his cup, and even slept in his arms. It was like a daughter to him."[b] But a neighbor with large flocks and herds decided to entertain a guest at the poor man's expense. He selfishly took the man's only lamb and slaughtered it.

Not knowing that this was a parable, David's pastoral sentiments were enraged. He demanded compensation fourfold and the rich man's death. Nathan then bluntly identified David as the guilty culprit with the memorable line, "You are the man!"[c] How far the king had come from the days when he had gently cared for the young of his father's flock.

The parable had its way with the king's conscience and David repented.

In the only other case where David apparently gives in to royal pretension, his shepherd's heart brings him to his senses. Near the end of his life he called for a census.[d] This may have been in preparation for war, taxation, or the organization of public labor. Or perhaps it was just for pride. Whatever the motive, it was out of line with God's will, and even the militant general Joab was repulsed by it. When the counting was complete, the Lord vowed to punish Israel.

---

a. Ps. 78:70–72 (NASB) b. 2 Sam. 12:3 c. 2 Sam. 12:7 d. 1 Chron. 21

Having realized his mistake, David pleaded for mercy. He was given three choices through the prophet Gad: three years of famine, three months of enemy raids, or three days of deadly plagues. David chose the third option, believing that God would be more merciful than his enemies. When the angel of the Lord came to Jerusalem, he relented. David then prayed, "Was it not I who ordered the fighting men to be counted? I am the one who has sinned and done wrong. *These are but sheep.* What have they done? O LORD my God, let your hand fall upon me and my family, but do not let this plague remain on your people."[a]

In this moment David realized that it was a shepherd's role to sacrifice himself for the sheep to live—not the other way around. At this very place where David returned to his senses the temple would one day stand.

Care of the young—the totally dependent and vulnerable among a flock—is a signature concern on a good shepherd's heart and the mark of a healthy community. An Asian pastor once told me that in his country foreign missionaries were evaluated on the basis of how they treated the children. Jesus continues to remind us, his disciples, that the young are more important than our well-intentioned agendas.[b]

a. 1 Chron. 21:17 b. Matt. 19:13-15

As we work among our flocks, do we find ourselves overlooking the physically young or giving special attention to them? Are abandoned children and relational orphans forgotten or looked after? Can we see past physical age and recognize adults who are developmentally delayed "infants" craving milk?[a] We need to be both strategic and gentle in our service. Casualties come to some that are "driven hard," especially in the name of ministry.

Caring shepherds are also attentive to their ewes. Are single parents and overburdened caregivers supported with competence and compassion? Healthy spiritual ewes, effectively reproducing newborns in the faith, need exceptional care. These mothers in the faith expend enormous effort bringing others to life and then months of nurture so the young can become independent.

We sometimes forget that mothers need to be mothered. Nurturers need to be nurtured. Life-givers need life poured into them. Shepherd leadership combines the sensitivities and the skills of a good midwife and nurse. *Leading means mothering.*

Moses once complained, "Did I conceive all these people? Did I give them birth? Why do you tell me to carry them in my arms, as a nurse carries an infant, to the land you promised on oath to their forefathers?"[b] God *did* call him to a maternal ministry; he was a midwife and nurse to the nation just as Deborah was a "mother in Israel."[c] Paul understood that this was a standard expectation for the church's shepherds: "As apostles of Christ...we were gentle among you, like a mother caring for her little children."[d]

Let's accept the call to be midwives and nurses.

---

a. 1 Cor. 3:1; Heb. 5:12-13 b. Num. 11:12 c. Judg. 5:7 d. 1 Thess. 2:6–7

*Rejoice with me, for I have found
my sheep which was lost!*

—Luke 15:6

Lost and Found

There are about one billion sheep in the world, but each one matters to a shepherd somewhere.

I asked Bedouin about losing sheep and hardly ever missed hearing a touching story that carried some remarkable sentiment. From the mountains surrounding ancient Petra, Ahmed responded with characteristic confidence: "Since 1984 I have never lost a sheep or goat that I didn't find again—dead or alive."

But then, with hesitation and obvious feeling, he continued, "Except one. And that one I can never forget. She is on my mind every night before I sleep." Although he had thousands of animals, he felt shamed as a shepherd that he could not account for one that was lost.

A happier story came from the Aref family in a small village near Karak, also in Jordan. Herding had been their family business for generations. In more recent history the men had taken government jobs, and Mrs. Aref now cared for their manageable flock of forty-five. The family joked that she brought in more income from the animal products than they did from their office jobs. She made wool-stuffed pillows and mattresses, dried cheeses, *laven* (clarified butter), and *labneh* (a cultured yogurt).

Another family joke was that Mrs. Aref loved her animals as much as—maybe more than—her children. She knew the animals quite intimately and was greatly affected by their needs. While we ate one of her sumptuous meals, they indulged me with a personal story about their beloved mother and her favorite animals.

One day, to her immense distress, Mrs. Aref lost track of one of her ewes. Because sheep regularly mingle with other flocks at common pastures during the day, she checked with her neighbors that night to see if the ewe had gone home with someone else. But none of them had seen the missing creature. She inquired among more distant neighbors over the next week, but no one had noticed a stray or found unidentified remains. Weeks turned into months without a sign of the missing ewe.

Then one day, two months later, a large flock came through the village led by a hired shepherd. As was still her habit, Mrs. Aref asked the young man if he had come across a lost sheep. As the words passed her lips, one of the ewes in the solid pack of passing sheep lifted her head, immediately recognizing the sound of her owner's voice. Mrs. Aref screamed with delight and rushed through the startled mass

to embrace her lost sheep. It didn't take long before the whole village heard the commotion and shared in the reunion. Her flock was now complete again.

A final story from a Syrian shepherd has the same happy ending. A couple of brothers searched through the night till they discovered the trail of their two missing sheep. When they came back to their village, their father was calling for them, "'Have you found them?' The answer we sent back to him, 'saved, both saved,' was enough to fill that little house of ours with great rejoicing. Rejoicing did I say? Why, every member of our family asked us to tell again and again the story of how our sheep were sought for, found, and saved."[1]

These accounts have a familiar ring to them. We all know the parable of the man with one hundred sheep who went in search of one that was lost until he found it.[a] The response was the same—everyone in the village celebrated over the sheep that was found. Jesus used this story to help his hearers appreciate the joy in heaven when one who was "lost" is saved. In God's kingdom, he was teaching, we should always "count by ones."[2]

I found another purpose for Jesus' story. Frequently dining with tax-collectors, prostitutes, and other "sinners," he was painting a picture of how God views those outside the formal membership of the community of faith. They are "lost"—a designation that reflects a profound perspective on their true identity. Like sheep, people wander off and lose their way. They need to be rescued and returned to the flock where they belong. They need to be "saved." The theologically shocking truth was that even the despised tax-collector Zacchaeus was a "true child of Abraham"[b] waiting to be found. The lost are "those Jesus misses most."[3]

---

a. Luke 15:3-7 b. Luke 19:9

Jesus was intent on reconnecting those who had become isolated, searching with resolve for each one "until he finds it."[a] His focused mission was "*to seek and to save the lost.*"[b] He called disciples to continue that mission, sending them out to retrieve the "lost sheep of Israel."[c] He also informed them of the broader scope of his mission: "I have other sheep...I must bring them also."[d]

One of the essential tasks of shepherd leadership is the arduous retrieval of those who—*for whatever reason*—have lost their way. Most don't even know that they're lost until it is too late. Anguish over the lost expresses itself in passionate intercession and determined action. I find this anguish too often missing in my own self-absorbed existence. It's easier to just let them go. I think, *They aren't interested in what I have to say anyway.*

The parable's searching shepherd provides a poignant vision of the evangelistic mission of the church's shepherds. *Leadership means looking for the lost.* Shepherd leaders feel comfortable in places where sheep get lost. We need to know our way around tough neighborhoods, vacant lots, bars, and homeless shelters.

---

a. Luke 15:4 b. Luke 19:10 c. Matt. 10:6 d. John 10:16

Attentive leaders notice those who are missing—not just the ones who are normally among us. Those who have never been in the flock are missed at the daily counting. Even if they resist initial attempts to bring them back, the shepherd knows that they need to come home where they truly belong. They need to be saved.

The "other sheep" Jesus was referring to include sub-cultures in our society that we may never have reached out to or prayed for. And people groups and nations that we may have only seen through the lenses of our media. At the climax of history the flock of God will include every tribe, tongue, language, and nation.[a] As a seminarian I remember praying regularly for Albania, the only known country then without a single Christian. Now there are many. The angels rejoiced over each one.

How much are we affected by those still missing? By some estimates, there are almost 3 billion individuals living without a clear understanding of the gospel.[4] Does the mental picture of "other sheep" have some flesh? As we reflect on the relentless, optimistic persistence of the Good Shepherd, let's allow his unyielding passion for the lost to fill our hearts again.

One final thought about lostness. As vital as evangelistic zeal is to the shepherd's role in Scripture, we must remember that the *shepherd* may also be lost. Following the story of the lost sheep in Luke 15 is the story of a lost coin and a lost son. We call this final story the "Parable of the Prodigal Son." Perhaps we should think of this touching account as the story of two lost sons. One went away physically and returned home to a new life as a son. The other didn't leave home, but he never shared his father's heart. Really, he was the more tragic of the two characters. He was lost at home. Paul warns all of us, "Test *yourselves* to see if you are in the faith; examine *yourselves!*"[b]

a. Rev. 7:9 b. 2 Cor. 13:5 (NASB)

I will gather those who have been scattered.

—Zephaniah 3:19

Gathering the Scattered

Hearing many stories about sheep that went astray, I was intrigued with how the strong sense of responsibility was inculcated in the young. Saíd, a Bedouin from the Sinai, helped answer the question with an unforgettable story. By the age of seven, his father regularly sent him out into the surrounding granite canyons of southern Sinai with their small flock of thirty goats for daily feeding. One day he returned at dusk with one goat missing. (Saíd had become distracted by the attention of a shepherd girl with another flock!) His father's response was swift and, to my mind, harsh: "Go back out and don't come home without it." Even though the goat had made its way back home by itself the next morning, Saíd's father didn't call for his son.

The young boy searched the mountains for two days.

When he returned home, frightened and embarrassed, his father made no apologies. Apparently this was the traditional way of learning responsibility for the family's flock. Wow!

As I thought about the young boy's experience (and the incredible challenge of keeping goats together), it was hard not to sympathize with him. But another story from Mrs. Aref revealed how important it is to take responsibility for animals, especially when they are separated and threatened.

One night a frightening storm in the Jordanian mountains caused the tents to collapse around the animals. In panic, the flocks ran helter-skelter into the black night. The hired shepherd panicked and ran too. With thunder and rain above and slick rocks underfoot, the family members climbed and called, tracking their dispersed flock. By the end of that exhausting dark and rain-filled night, the Arefs tracked the scattered animals and gathered them under temporary shelter.

In the morning they went searching for the hired hand who had deserted them in their hour of need. They were understandably angry! He was hiding behind the baker's oven in a nearby village, afraid they would take his life.

And they could have.

He had run when they needed him most.

With these stories in mind I now find it easier to understand the sentiment expressed in Ezekiel 34. God chastised the leaders of ancient Israel for not being shepherds. Like Saíd, distraction with their own concerns had led to neglect of the flock, a passive expression of abuse.

During the prophet Ezekiel's lifetime a storm of war came to God's flock, Israel. They would scatter, be taken advantage of, and many would perish. All because the shepherds were careless and self-centered. The prophet describes the consequences:

> So they were scattered because there was no shepherd, and when they were scattered they became food for all the wild animals. My

sheep wandered over all the mountains and on every high hill. They were scattered over the whole earth, and no one searched or looked for them...As a shepherd looks after his scattered flock when he is with them, so will I look after my sheep. I will rescue them from all the places where they were scattered on a day of clouds and darkness. (Ezek. 34:6–12)

Ezekiel was describing the *dispersion* of the Jews in the dark storm of their national exile.[1] The nation was literally scattered across the Babylonian empire. They had become *sheep without a shepherd,* a frequent designation for people without proper leadership.[2]

The Babylonian rulers themselves knew that a good king was "a shepherd who collects the dispersed."[3]

As a response to the plight of God's flock, the Divine Shepherd vows to remove the non-shepherds and to go in search of his lost sheep personally: "I will seek the lost, *gather the scattered,* bind up the broken and strengthen the sick."[a] What a passionate portrayal of God's intense commitment to his dispersed people.

a. Ezek. 34:16 (author's translation)

The personal arrival of this Shepherd came in the ministry of the Messiah Jesus. Seeing the crowds as sheep without a shepherd, he gathered them to himself. It's amazing how many times the word *gather* is used in the ministry of Jesus.[a] He purposefully surrounded himself with the exiles of Israel, forging a renewed community out of them.[4]

Jesus passed on this perspective to the leaders of the early church. In a letter addressed to "the twelve tribes scattered among the nations,"[b] James wrote to believers as displaced aliens in this world, encouraging them to live by faith here as temporary residents.

At the close of James's letter he addresses a sub-group of the dispersed who have deliberately chosen to scatter and wander from God's chosen path.[c] To this tendency he encourages a good shepherd's response: "My brothers, if one of you should wander from the truth and someone should bring him back, remember this: Whoever turns a sinner from the error of his way will save him from death and cover over a multitude of sins."[d]

We might begin our reflections on this topic with some introspection. Have *we* been wandering? One of my favorite hymns is Robert Robertson's *Come Thou Fount of Every Blessing*. The following lines come to me often:

> O to grace how great a debtor, daily I'm constrained to be!
> Let Thy goodness, like a fetter, Bind my wandering heart to Thee.
> *Prone to wander—LORD, I feel it—Prone to leave the God I love;*
> Here's my heart—O take and seal it, Seal it for Thy courts above.

As we turn our attention to our scattered sheep, let's remember Paul's words in Galatians 6:1: "Brothers, if someone is caught in a sin, you who are spiritual

a. Cf. Luke 8:4; 12:1 b. James 1:1 c. Cf. Ps. 95:10 d. James 5:19-20

should restore him gently. But watch yourself, or you also may be tempted." First we look inward with brutal honesty, and then move toward gentle restoration.

I suggest that we catalog the various ways people in our care wander off and get scattered. Some scatter seeking pleasure over one hill or another. Seeking pleasure in work, alcohol, gambling, or pornography has led some to serious addictions. These have drifted from view; they are struggling and trapped in physical or psychological prisons. A pastor friend confessed how his marriage was almost destroyed simply because of a few nights one week surfing pornography on the internet. He let his mind wander.

Others are pursuing seemingly harmless interests. They have "lost their first love" for the Divine Shepherd. Among like-minded sheep they toy with New Age philosophy or flock compulsively around money-making endeavors. Some are scattering because of fear, running away from the very support systems that would help them. They are jumpy with rumors of change, hints of problems, a rumble in the sky. Do we see these little groups scuttling out of sight? They become homeless sometimes by choice, sometimes by circumstance. And the word from our Father who sends us out is, "Don't come home without them."

He restores my soul; my cup overflows.

—Psalm 23:3,5

Satisfaction and Restoration

One of my favorite experiences in Jordan was on an October day in the shepherds' fields without an interpreter. Early in my "field education," I was hoping to learn first just by watching, listening, and following. In the morning my son Jesse and I followed a shepherd who was hired by several families in Ismakhiah to take care of their respective flocks. He handled about two hundred animals.

Later in the day we met up in a large valley with several other hired shepherds who let their flocks of similar size graze together away from the town. I watched intently and copiously scribbled notes. I accumulated countless questions that would hopefully be answered in the shepherd's tent that night. Most importantly, I was gaining distinct impressions about the routines and rhythms of flock life.

One of the images imprinted on my mind from that day was the scene of a few sheep, happily snuggled next to each other on the ground for an afternoon rest. Others were huddled or "flocking" nearby. But the ones on the ground were peculiarly peaceful. It took a good bit of the day for the flock to get used to us, but by this time I was able to move slowly toward them, sit down nearby, and take their picture.

What makes the impression so memorable is the lack of motion and restlessness that is so common. Sheep are usually on the move as they graze. They are easily provoked by other sheep or goats and typically shuttle around, clustering in their cliques. They panic easily when an unknown person is around. They seem overly sensitive to any changes in the environment. But when there is nothing and no one bothering them, and their stomachs are full, they just lie down and ruminate in contented satisfaction.[1]

While the sheep rested, the shepherds spontaneously began to play music on handmade instruments. They sang some songs and danced a bit, providing Jesse and me with some unexpected entertainment.[2] There was such a natural correspondence between the carefree respite for the sheep and the shepherds. I couldn't help but think of King David who probably composed some of his psalms when he was a young shepherd.

The scene of satisfied sheep is ironic in a way. The desert is a place of desolation and depravation, where all life is drawn toward death. But good shepherds can provide life-sustaining gifts for their flocks in this kind of place. And when they do, we see a perfect picture of rejuvenating satisfaction. It was in precisely this kind of region that God chose to self-reveal as provider and sustainer. "For forty years," Moses reminded the Israelites, "you *lacked nothing.*"[a]

When Israel faced another kind of wilderness—the desolation of exile—God promised through Jeremiah, "I will bring Israel back and they will graze and *be satisfied.*"[b] These images remind us of how the famous Shepherd Psalm begins: "Because the LORD is my Shepherd, I lack nothing."[c]

The verb used in Jeremiah for bringing Israel back is the same one used in Psalm 23 for "restoring" my soul.[3] It seems to me that biblical restoration involves returning to a place of divine provision where comprehensive care is available and where life can be restored.[4] The sequence in the psalm is suggestive: "He makes me lie down in green pastures, he leads me beside the 'waters of rest,'[5] he restores my soul."[d] The restoration the psalmist so desperately longs for comes when his deepest needs are met. In lush, nutritious pastures. By still streams. After the turbulence has passed. In the complete security of the Shepherd's presence. There the Shepherd mends the hurting soul. There the sheep's well-being and spiritual resources are regenerated. There "my cup overflows."[e]

Among the gospel writers, Mark especially notes the frequent incidence of Christ's restorative ministry in the desert. He understands this outreach as the continued pastoral care of the God who formerly nurtured Israel in the same environment. In Mark 6:31 Jesus entices his disciples to share some solitude with him after their first missionary journey. The crowds had been pressing in on them, they were hungry, and dusk was approaching. He invited them to "come away by yourselves to a desert place, and rest awhile."[6]

---

a. Deut. 2:7 b. Jer. 50:19 c. Ps. 23:1 (author's translation) d. Ps. 23:2–3 e. Ps. 23:5

But the crowds followed them to their retreat. Understandably, the disciples suggested to their rabbi that the people be sent away to get some food for themselves—and they could be left alone. We've looked at what transpires briefly already, but there's more to discover.

Jesus saw the crowd not simply as a needy mob, but rather as sheep without a shepherd.[a] He challenged the disciples to feed them. All five thousand families! Ludicrous, of course, from a human perspective. But the Lord who had provided manna for forty years was here to provide a meal for a hungry flock again. And he wanted his disciples to have a hand in it all. Along with that, he wanted to show them that the meal he was about to provide would be *more than enough*.

As the disciples participated in the miracle of multiplying fish and loaves, they each found themselves at the end of the day with a basket full of *leftovers*! Imagine thousands of people reclining on the wilderness hillsides, stuffed to satisfaction, and twelve disciples in a kind of tired, bewildered, delightful stupor, lying down next to their Lord—with all the leftovers. Ruminating.

"And they all ate and were satisfied"[b]—five thousand families *and twelve men*. I see this second vivid image alongside the picture of the sheep outside Ismakhiah taken that autumn day.

Satisfaction involves having genuine needs met and depleted resources replenished. In light of the Shepherd's example, let's probe more deeply into the ways we might effectively satisfy the needs of others. We are whole people who have such a variety of needs: physical, emotional, psychological, intellectual, relational, and spiritual. The first question is how we assess needs in our places of ministry. By intuition and assumptions or with real data? Do we really *want* to know the

a. Mark 6:34 b. Mark 6:42

extent of the needs? What kind of needs do we seek to meet? Only "spiritual" needs?

Reflect for a moment on the Hebrew notion of restoration as returning. This might involve the restoration of marriage—a return to its former state. For some it might involve a return to a better state, *a restoration to God's ideal.* Many have never experienced a healthy marriage or family life. Some have only known dysfunction in their places of employment. How can we recreate God's ideal?

Return might mean an inward journey to an extraordinary kind of rest and rejuvenation. Perhaps restoration brings to mind a certain place (near water or in the mountains), a physical state (stillness or solitude), or a certain activity (Scripture meditation or listening to music). Worship rises freely from the satisfied hearts of those whose needs are tended to.

I watched a prominent pastor become speechless when, after a stimulating presentation to other leaders on his ambitious vision, he was asked, "Do you give your people a chance to rest?" At its best this question was not simply about "compensation time" or vacation benefits. It was about promoting a rhythm of restoration and rejuvenation for ourselves and those we lead. It was about the quality of ministry that characterized the Shepherd who said, "Come to me, all you who are weary and burdened, and I will give you rest. Take my yoke upon you and learn from me, for I am gentle and humble in heart, and you will find rest for your souls. For my yoke is easy and my burden is light."[a] Like the disciples on that mountainside, we can enjoy the Lord's rest even while serving his people.

"He restores my soul. *My cup overflows.*"[b]

---

a. Matt. 11:28–30 b. Ps. 23:3,5

Your staff brings me comfort

—Psalm 23:4

The Staff

Two simple wooden implements became symbols of the shepherd's roles among his flock, two extensions of his presence among them. The rod and staff each had its purpose. We'll examine the rod on another day when we consider protection and discipline. The staff is the symbol of care, and a suitable emblem for the provider's profile we've been sketching. With it a shepherd provides gentle assistance, direction, and encouragement at critical moments.

The staff is tall enough to lean on and is often curved at the top. It is made from a long, straight branch, with the "crook" traditionally formed by heating and bending the still-green end, and rubbing it with oil. The crook is useful for pulling branches down for goats, rescuing animals trapped just out of reach, and for nudging newborns to their mothers. The staff has endless uses, not the least of which is for the shepherd to lean on while he attentively watches his flock. I came to see the staff as an extension of the shepherd's caring and guiding presence.

One of the critical moments when a staff is needed is during lambing. Though shepherds are often involved quite physically during this process, the staff allows them to keep just enough distance to prompt nature to take its course with minimal interference. Phillip Keller describes the interaction beautifully:

I have watched skilled shepherds moving swiftly with their staffs among thousands of ewes that were lambing simultaneously. With deft but gentle strokes the newborn lambs are lifted with the staff and placed side by side with their dams. It is a touching sight that can hold one spellbound for hours.[1]

When a mother rejects her newborn, shepherds resort to a variety of strategies to get the lambs accepted by other ewes. If a ewe has had a stillborn, they might cloak an orphaned lamb with the skin of the dead one. With the constant prodding of the staff the ewe is faced with the needy stray concealed in a familiar smell. Lambs may appear to be independent, walking soon after birth, but they are vitally dependent on this initial bonding with their mother, whether surrogate or natural.

The staff is also extremely important in rescue operations. Sheep have a way of getting caught in pits, fences, bushes, and crevices. They can get stuck in mud or, worse, swept off by a flash flood. The staff becomes an extension of a shepherd's arm, reaching carefully around the isolated creature and pulling it back to safety.

This useful instrument can also guide sheep through a pass, lightly pointing out the way with a shoulder tap. The staff gently separates sheep from each other when tension arises, and it brings sheep together when they need to be. A simple stick becomes a tangible, tactile extension of the shepherd's voice, expressing his concerns or directions throughout the day.

The most interesting use of the staff is, in Keller's words, to "be in touch."[2] Walking side by side, almost as if holding hands, a shepherd may simply lay the staff against the side of a special animal. Special perhaps because it needs more frequent affirmation. Or because it is most likely to wander. Or it might just be a favorite.

In the world of the Bible the staff was a symbol for a person's leadership. The ancient Egyptian hieroglyph for ruler or prince was a pictorial representation of the shepherd's staff. Moses' staff was the instrument by which Pharaoh was forced to witness God's power.[a] The budding of Aaron's staff was supernatural confirmation of God's choice of his family line for priestly leadership.[b] But most often, this simple, common shepherd's instrument was the identifying signature of individuals, a physical expression of their unique identities.[c] In fact, when God first called Moses, the empowering of his staff confirmed the call.[d] His shepherd's staff took on a spiritual dimension.

With this background I find it more than coincidental that Jesus sent his disciples out for ministry saying, "Take nothing for the journey except a staff."[e]

The staff helps me think about "indirect shepherding"—what we do at arms length. Newborns in the faith need to be attached to a nurturing mentor or care group for support and counsel. They need to be prodded by a shepherd's "staff" into a good match where they can bond and flourish. Shepherds cannot personally remain involved with each one. They get the relationships started. How appropriate that we call our helpers "staff."

photo courtesy of Dr. James C. Martin. The Cairo Museum

a. Exod. 7:10 et al b. Num. 17 c. Gen. 38:18, 25 d. Exod. 4:2ff. e. Mark 6:8

We also need the shepherd's rescuing staff. Like sheep, people get stuck. I remember the first time we tried to help a single mom in welfare housing. Our problem-solving instincts ran into the entrenched inner-city web of despondency, abuse, poor self-esteem, and a maze of unhealthy habits and relationships. She needed child care, educational support, marriage counseling, job training, advocates, friends, and a welcoming church. The staff was all these tangible means of aid.

We all can get trapped and need to be rescued. A dreamy-eyed runaway is now a cynical hideaway. A middle-aged professional ditches his job and wife for a romantic mirage. An earnest pastor finds himself in his fourth pastorate wondering why he is being asked, once again, to turn in his resignation. A mother is home-bound with the care of a disabled child or elderly parent, paralyzed in a world turned gray with depression and despair. These and many others need a staff stretched out to them.

People are stuck in debt, caught in compulsive behaviors, trapped in prostitution. They are wedged in a crevice almost out of sight, with desperate feelings of insecurity, confused ideas of their own sexuality, or a completely broken moral compass.

When we get hung up, our only hope is for someone with sincere interest and gentle persistence to reach over the gap with a staff, to reach out and rescue us. The staff may be an email, a phone call, or a basket of flowers on a doorstep or desk.

The most subtle use of the staff is to "be in touch" with someone who may just need a word of encouragement or a hug. These are ways of saying, "Everything will be OK" or "I'm right beside you." These statements echo two of the most common messages God speaks to people in the Bible: "Do not be afraid" and "I am with you." The staff represents these messages. A post-it note on the computer screen. A treat left in the lunch bag. A surprise party. A well-thought-out job review. A call on the anniversary of a loved one's death. A passage of Scripture read at someone's bedside.

We all need tangible emblems of a shepherd's care so that we can say with assurance, "Your staff brings me comfort."[a]

---

a. Ps. 23:4

And the sheep recognize his voice and come to him,
and he calls his own sheep by name.

—John 10:3

Named and Known

After returning from a year of field interviews, I continued reading shepherd stories, occasionally from other regions in the world. The following account comes from a book about herders in India. In it I find an authentic sentiment expressed by so many of the shepherds I had met personally in the Middle East.

> Three weeks ago, when we camped near the Kaneda train station, Ghewarji fell asleep on guard duty in the night. The poor man had just returned from his home and is still recovering from all the work his wife made him do...In the morning Modaramji found seven sheep missing from his flock. You ask how he knew exactly seven were missing out of more than three hundred? Well, Moda knows all his sheep by name...Don't smile. Each sheep has a name, and when Moda calls they come running. And the same is true for all shepherds who are their mothers' sons.[1]

Sheep know they belong to a shepherd. They are named, known, and counted every day.[2] Naming usually takes place soon after birth, especially if there is some distinguishing characteristic. Picture Spotty, Brownie, Fluffy Ears, or Short Tail. Others are named for the birth place or the birthing experience. So, one might be Hebron, another Tough-coming. As with names for humans, some are changed because of a critical event or an identity that emerges over time. Think of The Wanderer or The Obstinate One.

Naming is a powerful, tangible expression of the shepherd's intimate bond that begins at birth and grows through an animal's tenure with a flock. Once you begin to fathom how many times an animal may have been counted, checked, carried, nursed back to health, rescued, protected, milked, and shorn, it dawns on you why Bedouin always say, "They are family."

Consider the remarkably intimate knowledge of a shepherd for members of this extended family:

The mothers, which number 51 (42 sheep and 9 goats) were kept back from the lambs by Faláh and Salim, while Nasir began to call them by name, and as each was allowed to come up Nasir slipped the noose off the young one's neck and gave it to the mother. He knew every mother and every lamb. *An astonishing thing was that he called up each ewe and picked out her lamb in complete darkness...*All through the process of loosing the lambs, calling up the mothers and handing the baby to its dam to suckle, he was calling out name after name amidst the din of mothers' "baaing" and lambs crying for their food. To me it was pandemonium; to Nasir and Faláh, everyday procedure...*He could recognize each mother and each baby by the feel with his eyes shut. All were black, but by feeling heads and backs he knew by touch which was which.*[3]

In an interview I had with Abu-Munir I asked him how much contact he had with his flock of two thousand. Here was an affluent man, with two wives each in a separate home and hired help overseeing different sub-flocks. He clearly didn't need to be out in the fields. His answer surprised me, "I am with the sheep every day. In the summer I sleep outside with them too."[4]

Then he said something even more surprising, "If I weren't with them every day, I shouldn't be their shepherd." What a bond between shepherd and sheep! He was concerned that he would lose touch with them if he were not out among them every day.

I met two other shepherds, one man over eighty, and a woman over one hundred (!), both of whom insisted on keeping a small flock. Though each had pressure from family to give up their animals, the response from both was the same: "I can't live without them. They are family."

Caring and invested shepherds like these remind me of the poor man in Nathan's parable who "had nothing except one little ewe lamb which he bought and nourished. And it grew up together with him and his children. It would eat of his bread and drink of his cup and lie in his bosom, and was like a daughter to him."[a] Flocks become members of the family.

Nathan's fictional character is like the Divine Shepherd in Psalm 23. In this poem a subtle movement transpires. Indirect statements *about* the shepherd (*he* makes me lie down...*he* leads me...*he* restores...*he* guides...for *his* name's sake) shift to direct statements *to* the shepherd (*You* are with me; *Your* rod and *Your* staff, they comfort me. *You* prepare a table before me... *You* anoint my head). This timeless psalm by a single "sheep" expresses the assurance and security of being

a. 2 Sam. 12:3

known, cared for, and counted. Jeremiah predicts a day when, "In the cities of the hill country..., in the land of Benjamin, in the environs of Jerusalem, the flocks shall

again pass under the hands of the one who numbers them."[a] In John 10 the Good Shepherd "calls his own sheep by name and leads them out...and the sheep follow him because they know his voice."[b]

Have we fully realized the security and assurance that come with being named and known? God's intimate knowledge of each individual in his flock began before we were even born. He shaped us in our mothers' wombs and ordained the

---

a. Jer. 33:13 b. John 10:3–4

days of our lives. He even keeps track of the hairs on our heads.[a] His thoughts about us are countless.[b]

What kind of knowledge do we have of those in our flocks? Their names are only the beginning of their distinct identities. The people we serve cannot become for us merely "staff," "laity," "members," "students," or "the kids." Those roles are extrinsic to each one's primary identity. Our flocks are collections of persons—individuals with feelings, aspirations, convictions, needs, and names. They have perspective-shaping histories and unique callings. Have we fully appreciated what impacts, affects, and motivates each one? Does every individual get resourced and disciplined in a tailored way? Is each one given the right conditions to thrive? Do they follow us like we follow the Good Shepherd—because they know they are known?

A senior pastor I respect a great deal tells his pastoral staff regularly, "I don't want to find you in your offices very often." He expects them to be out with the sheep every day cultivating relationships and building intimacy. If our churches are true expressions of "God's household,"[c] the shepherds will know names. "Know well the faces of your flocks."[d]

a. Matt. 10:30 b. Ps. 139:13–18 c. Eph. 2:19; 1 Tim. 3:15; 1 Pet. 4:17 d. Prov. 27:23 (author's translation)

PROTECTION

I will raise up shepherds to tend them,
and they will no longer be afraid or terrified.

—Jeremiah 23:4

PROTECTION

I found shepherds constantly referring to the need for protection, since a wilderness environment is both a source of nourishment and a hub of hazards. Shepherds have to exploit the life-giving assets of these desolate settings while protecting their flocks from ever-present deadly threats. They described their dogs and rifles and the security of their pens. And I heard story after story about hyenas, panthers, wolves, and thieves. The geography and climate also conspire against the welfare of a herd: the sand, the sun, the wind, and the floods.

One of the ironies of shepherding in the wilderness is that while flock animals are physiologically suited to arid wastelands, they are completely defenseless in these remote regions. Sheep don't have sharp teeth or claws. Their eyesight is limited to between ten and fifteen yards. The animals' only natural defense is their instinct to huddle or "flock" together. Isolation spells sure ruin. The only reliable source of security comes from the shepherd's presence. *A flock cannot be left alone!*

The sheep's utter dependence on shepherds is commonly observed. More striking is their passive submission to human leadership, even during branding, sheering, and slaughter. While this remarkable behavior can easily lead to abuse, good shepherds view this temperament as worthy of respect. The Sarakatsani herders say, "Sheep are docile, enduring, and pure...They suffer in silence. To match this purity and passive courage shepherds ought to be fearless and devoted guardians."[1]

The more I heard shepherds refer to courage, the more I appreciated their role as protectors. I found a characteristic pride among herders who had weathered storms for their flocks, fought hand-to-hand with wild predators, and slept out in the open, ready to defend their livestock at the risk of their own lives. One Jordanian Bedouin bragged about his brother during an interview, "Najida is strong of heart. He has slept in a cave with a hyena!" Another shepherd just showed me his hands to prove how many times he had been bitten by vipers and other wild animals.

This treacherous life is too much for the faint of heart. One boy confessed, "There was too much danger for me every day. The dunes are dangerous. The jungle by the river is dangerous. All the hyenas live in the dunes or in the jungle. Also maybe a thief comes and I don't see him."[2] You can empathize with the young shepherd's terror. Once the darkness falls, anyone can panic. But should he run, a whole herd will become victims.

When the psalmist prays, "Though I walk through the valley of deadly shadows, I will fear no harm,"[a] his confidence is grounded in the fearless courage and vigilance of his Divine Shepherd. Though green pastures and still waters are essential for the sheep's health and well-being, the provider must also be a trustworthy protector for the dependent animal's survival. We often think of David as shepherd poet, but before he became king he was recognized as a valiant warrior as well.[b]

---

a. Ps. 23:4 (author's translation) b. 1 Sam. 16:18

I was surprised by how many ancient kings described themselves as shepherd warriors. Consider the words of Neo-Assyrian King Assurnasirpal I, a figure roughly contemporary with David:

> Without rival among the princes of the four quarters, *the wonderful shepherd*, who fears not opposition, the mighty flood who has no conqueror, the king who has brought into subjection those that were not submissive to him, the mighty hero who treads on the neck of his foe, *who tramples all enemies under foot*, who shatters the might of the haughty.[3]

In ancient Greece shepherding was associated metaphorically with military leadership more than with any other role. The major writers of the classical period depicted Greek commanders frequently as shepherds, though the pastoral image was occasionally qualified with references to intimacy and concern for the men in one's charge. Shepherd generals were tender toward their own "flocks" and fierce protectors of their homelands. Apparently, they found this combination of roles natural and congruent.

The more I studied these texts together with Scripture, the more I realized that this combination was biblical. God's people were often threatened by invading armies. Worse, they were abused and harassed by their own leaders. God promised to appoint shepherd leaders over his people so "they will no longer be afraid or terrified."[a]

We've already seen the setting for Jesus' declaration of his identity as the Good Shepherd in John 10. His compassion for a blind man led to conflict with religious leaders he would implicitly implicate as thieves, hirelings, and even wolves. Only Israel's legitimate Leader could be trusted to protect his sheep. He would do no less than lay his life down for them.

---

a. Jer. 23:4[4]

The Good Shepherd would be more direct in other speeches. In a series of prophetic woes, he castigated self-serving leaders as a "brood of vipers" whose intent was only harm.[a] Jesus was a tenacious prophetic shepherd who challenged Israel's leadership when he found the crowds "harassed and helpless, like sheep without a shepherd."[b]

In this second segment of our journey we'll be trying to balance nurturing and compassionate provision with vigilant and courageous protection. Each role calls for a different sentiment and posture. One calls for a soft heart, the other a "strong heart." We'll learn to be gentle as doves *and* shrewd as serpents. We'll be called to care in the day *and* watch in the night.

Some of us prefer mercy to justice, grace to law, the staff to the rod. Others prefer the opposite. But, as shepherds, we need to occupy both roles comfortably. The parents who tuck their children into bed with a story, a prayer, and a gentle kiss are the same parents who check the alarm system, lock the doors, and respond swiftly if the dog barks. We understand intuitively that love expresses itself in both ways. Similarly, shepherding involves our God-given stewardship in tangible expressions of nurture and protection.

I've discovered this balance to be missing in Christian communities. Sometimes a board discussion will avoid sensitive issues because someone's feelings may get hurt. Yet the fate of our members hangs on our decisions. Shepherding requires us at times to lobby and advocate with resolve and to organize efforts against popular opinion. Shepherding requires us to "speak up for those who cannot speak for themselves."[c] Ultimately, shepherding requires an identification with our flock that leads to personal risk and sacrifice.

---

a. Matt. 23:33 b. Matt. 9:36 c. Prov. 31:8

Rabbi Leo Baeck was determined to help his fellow Jews in Germany during the Holocaust. He *voluntarily* admitted himself into a concentration camp. When activists among the Allied countries tried to arrange for a prisoner swap to release Baeck, they were told, "Your mission is in vain; if the man is such as you have described him, *he will never desert his flock.*"

May we all aspire to such an expression of shepherd leadership.

The LORD will guard you from all harm;
he will watch over your life.

—Psalm 121:7

While Shepherds Watch Their Flocks

𝄞 I met Amir, a sociable young shepherd, near Arad in southern Israel. He described the differences between village shepherds and desert shepherds such as himself: "We know the environment best because we live out here. We hear and see and sense things others do not. That's why the government hires us as guides." I'd heard incredible stories about Bedouin trackers who could find fugitives or lost animals or secret water sources in what appears to the rest of us as blank wilderness wasteland.

Amir explained that the ability to "see" what's not always visible is important when they choose new pastures. A *baheth* (inspector) would go ahead of the flocks on a camel and check for sufficient water and pasturage. More importantly, he would survey the area for possible hiding places for thieves, evidence of predators, natural shelters for protection, and caverns or drop-offs where animals could get hurt. The *baheth* would also have to discern if there were any other herders within range who might contest their relocation. Pasture theft is common. In Amir's world, "It's not who's there first, but who's strongest that counts."

Once a flock makes a major move, the need for informed, intuitive sight only increases. Shepherds spend a great deal of their time watching their flocks. At first this activity looks like passive inactivity (for which shepherds are occasionally criticized), but watchfulness involves continuous surveillance and active attention to what is happening...and constant concern over what might happen. You can't afford losses due to a "failure of imagination."[1]

I have sometimes asked shepherds what they look for when I see their intense gaze follow the movement of their flocks. What experience, what knowledge, what concerns lie behind that lingering look while they pause on their staff or stroll among their herds? Their active minds constantly take inventory: looking out for human and animal threats; assessing the weather, vegetation, and supplies; checking for signs of dehydration, disease, and anxiety; inspecting the mothers, the young, and the sick; and periodically counting bodies. They constantly question: Which animals need to be separated today? Which ones should stay back tomorrow? Will this one's hoof heal? Why is that ewe giving so little milk? Will that one give birth to twins? Is it the final year for that buck?

The watchful eye is not only taking stock of detailed information. Shepherds sometimes stand at a distance to see the "big picture." They may be intuiting the mood of the flock or reconsidering a major move in light of what they see. This kind of sight is a matter of perception, insight, instinct, and vision. These traits are essential for those involved in "oversight."

I did some research on the role of watching in the Bible. The Hebrew verb *shamar*, typically translated "watch," can mean "guard" or "oversee." Shepherds are watchmen and guards over the flock, the ones who oversee them.[2] At night their primary duty is to protect the animals under their care from thieves and animal predators.

As I searched the pages of Scripture, I found biblical writers quite naturally using watching or oversight as an expression of shepherd-like leadership. In Psalm 121 *shamar* is used six times in eight verses to describe God's pastoral protection in life's wildernesses. Peter, quoting Isaiah, reminds his readers that, "You were all like sheep going astray," rescued by "the Shepherd and *Overseer* of your souls."[a] Having set the standard, God judges reckless shepherds who do not "look after" the flock in their care.[b]

As undershepherds, elders are called to, "*Keep watch* over yourselves and all the flock of which the Holy Spirit has made you *overseers*. Be shepherds of the church of God, which he bought with his own blood."[c] Though the Greek term for overseer (*episkopos*) used here is often translated "bishop"[d] (a technical designation for an ecclesiastical position), its primary meaning is functional. It refers to those who look after or oversee the flock. Attentive watchmen garner the trust of both the sheep and the Head Shepherd.[e]

a. 1 Pet. 2:25 (cf. Isa. 53:6) b. Jer. 23:2 c. Acts 20:28 d. cf. Phil. 1:1; 1 Tim. 3:2; Titus 1:7 e. John 10:3

To "look after" a flock, "look out" for dangers, to "look in on" and "watch over" people, and "oversee" their well-being...this is a central and ceaseless function of shepherding. Paul says in 1 Thessalonians 5:6, "So then, let us not be like others, who are asleep, but let us be watchful and self-controlled."[3] Scripture's best example is the Divine Overseer: "He who watches over Israel will neither slumber nor sleep."[a]

Leadership in any organization—not least in the church—requires the capacity to do many tasks well. But at the center of the leader's role is something more subtle and subjective—discerning, attentive oversight. *Leading means watching.* It requires the ability to see and sense things like a Bedouin *baheth*. This capacity is necessary whether we are pastors or parents, CEOs or coaches, classroom teachers or individual mentors.

Leadership means paying attention to the well-being of members and staff, to trends in morale, signs of unease, and evidence of emerging hazards. Sometimes only the subtlest changes in flock behavior suggest distress, disagreement, or alarm. Who, at the expense of personal health, may be working too hard? Who might be hiding in ineffective busyness? Who might be suffering under bullying and abuse? Enemies may be both visible and invisible. Can we see them? Are we watching for them? Like trained counselors, leaders need to develop that extra sense to "see" what people often communicate without words.

As leaders we also need to think more carefully about the impact of change. Like a *baheth*, we need to scout out a new area and carefully prepare our flocks for a major transition.

One senior elder handed in his resignation after many years because, in his words, "All this business keeps me from shepherding the flock." His frustration was

a. Ps. 121:4

that time spent "in the tent" was at the expense of time *looking after* the people under his care. Watching his flock was the reason he was an elder in the first place.

Are we carefully watching our flocks or have we made the assumption that they can take care of themselves?

One final thought about watching. Because leadership is so demanding we need to make it easy for shepherds when we are the sheep they watch.

> Obey your leaders and submit to them, for they keep watch over your souls as those who will give an account. Let them do this with joy and not with grief. (Heb. 13:17, NASB)[a]

---

a. Cf. I Thes. 5:12–13; I Cor. 16:16

*I know that after I leave, savage wolves will come
in among you and will not spare the flock*

—Acts 20:29

Recognizing the Wolves

As the desert's daylight yields to dusky shadows, our shepherd hosts grow alert and perceptibly anxious. The wilderness is now a threatening place. Eyes scan the darkening horizon. Ears strain for hints of approaching danger. The conversation around the fire is disrupted by the sounds of distant movement.

Night arrives full of threats, most of which are rarely visible and barely audible. Now is the time when hyenas emerge from their caves. Jackals and panthers rouse. And the most cunning and persistent predators silhouette the ridges.

Wolves.

The evening rituals of counting and enclosing the flock in a pen near the tent by this time have already taken place. Sometimes sheep and goats are tied together under the tent. This nightly proximity provides warmth and, more importantly, safety from wolves. Once the flocks are secured, the contest begins. There is no margin for carelessness. The enemy is cunning, daring, and effective, especially when driven by cold and hunger. The inevitable is stated by another observer: "In camps high on the mountains shepherds stay awake throughout the night shouting, whistling, and slinging stones in all directions, while the dogs bark themselves hoarse. These precautions are fully justified as *wolves cause continual losses.*" [1] These losses are common enough to justify the Arab proverb, "At the end of the night the cries are heard." [2]

The desert is the natural home for both flock and pack. [3] While shepherds watch their flocks, so do the wolves. It is a nightly match of watching, waiting, and wits. Another Arab proverb acknowledges the inevitable result of negligence: "If onto a land of claws and fangs one sets to graze his bleating fold, and o'er them does not keep his watch, *he hands the wolf his crook to hold.*" [4]

Creeping around a fold at night, a pack of shrewd wolves working together can easily remove several choice sheep—especially those isolated from the flock. Lambs are often taken without the sound of a sheep's bleat or a dog's bark. A spooked young shepherd cries for mercy in the dark: "Spare my kids, O Wolf, and spare my mother-goats, nor harm me for that I am so little to tend so large a flock."[5] Muním, another shepherd, admitted, "Maybe if I was alone with the flock and two or three came, I'd just let them take one sheep and go."[6]

On a good night the wolves lose the battle. When the dawn arrives, they give a distinct, haunting howl. They will wait patiently until the next night.

Jesus compared himself to a good shepherd who wouldn't run in the presence of a snarling wolf.[a] During the New Testament period a hired shepherd was expected to defend the flock against a wolf. However, if—as Muním feared—he was confronted with several wolves, he was allowed to run for his own safety.[7]

The instinct to avoid confrontation is understandable, especially in the darkness of a desert night. However, the results of self-protective passivity are catastrophic. Jesus said, "Then the wolf attacks the flock and scatters it."[b] Chaos compounds itself in the darkness. The picture Jesus paints in John 10 echoes the extended parable in Ezekiel 34. There God's scattered sheep, separated from their guardians, became ready meat for desert carnivores.[c]

Culturally familiar with shepherd ways, biblical writers used the designation *wolves* for human predators that destroy communities *from within*. They might play the role of political[d] or judicial leaders "who leave nothing for the morning."[e] Most commonly they are deceitful teachers. Jesus warned, "Watch out for false prophets. They come to you in sheep's clothing, but inwardly they are ferocious wolves."[f]

Teachers have unique influence in a community. They can lead to truth or *mis*-lead to error. Jesus sent his disciples out to preach and teach as "sheep among wolves."[g] To do so he insisted that they combine dove-like innocence with serpent-like shrewdness.[h]

---

a. John 10:12 b. John 10:12 c. Ezek. 34:8 d. Ezek. 22:27 e. Zeph. 3:3 f. Matt. 7:15 g. Matt. 10:16
h. Matt. 10:16

Paul was sure that the church would continue to be vulnerable to cunning, deceptive, and highly persuasive wolves who "secretly slip in" among God's flock.[a] He warned members of his young congregations not to be "deceived with fine-sounding arguments," lest anyone literally *carry you off* "through philosophy and empty deceit."[b] As Paul prepared for his final good-byes to the elders in Ephesus, he warned:

> Be shepherds of the church of God, which he bought with his own blood. *I know that after I leave, savage wolves will come in among you and will not spare the flock.* Even from your own number men will arise and distort the truth in order to draw away disciples after them. *So be on your guard!* (Acts 20:29–31a)

A few years ago I heard a minister tell a group of peers a troubling story. One night he found his agitated youth pastor at the front door of his home, asking for unconditional love and protection before "I tell you something important." The pastor instinctively answered, "You know that, no matter what, you'll have my protection." But the horrifying reality was that the youth pastor had been molesting minors on church property—perhaps even the pastor's own daughters![8] Imagine making open-ended promises to a predator! This wolf needed to be exposed rather than protected.

When I heard this story I wondered, *How can we empower and trust others and "give them space" to do their work, yet without leaving them so unaccountable?* My motto now is, "Trust and verify."

a. Jude 4 b. Col. 2:4, 8

One associate minister called me after their pastor's moral failure had ripped the church in half, with the media gathering like flies. He asked, "Does seminary teach people when to call the police on your pastor?!"

In any community malicious intent is not only possible, but likely. Shepherd leadership calls for a realistic, cautious—even suspicious—outlook that expects and recognizes patient, persistent predators infiltrating an otherwise naïve community. Most of us would prefer not to think of being stalked, but we are. Shepherd leadership requires backbone to name, confront, and chase the wolves away. These actions take an incredible emotional toll on the shepherd. Those of us who have made the hard call when we were sure someone was dangerous have often suffered with a reputation for "crying wolf."

Wolves prowl the edges of every community. A young pastor's leadership is hamstrung by a deacon's spouse who doesn't even attend church services. A talk show host carries passive lambs to a den of generic spirituality where they lose their souls. A college professor teaches agnosticism eloquently, leaving childhood faith in ruins.

Is it possible that nobody sees these atrocities coming? A vigilant shepherd stays alert through the watches of the night, resisting the temptation to assume all is well. When we sense the approach of cunning wolves, we can't simply roll over and pretend they'll go away.

He lies in wait like a lion to catch the helpless.

—Psalm 10:9

Facing the Lions

Deep in the Sinai, Basim expressed his hatred for tigers because they may recklessly destroy dozens of animals, yet take only one for food. You could almost forgive them for satisfying their hunger, but carnage seems their game. Other shepherds despise the panthers most, or the hyenas. Many of the men describe physical tangles with these beasts. They unassumingly accepted this as a vocational hazard. "It goes with being a shepherd," Kamal told me with obvious pride. "I've been bitten, stung, and attacked by everything out there. I'm afraid of nothing and nothing hurts me anymore." He had not, however, faced the revered, archetypal enemy of shepherds. The lion.

Until recently many large and powerful predators lived in the lands of the Bible: lions, bears, tigers, panthers, hyenas, and leopards. Shepherds would often face these in hand-to-hand combat. Losing animals to dangerous desert carnivores was a begrudged expectation in the ancient world. Jacob reminded Laban that while he was guarding his uncle's flocks, he bore many losses personally, whether they were taken by day or by night.[a] One might chase a raiding lion away only to find gruesome evidence of a missing animal. Hired shepherds who lost a sheep or goat to a wild

---

a. Gen. 31:39

animal were exempt from penalty so long as they could provide such remains as proof.

Lions spend their lives engaged in two primary activities: sleeping after a meal and looking for a meal. They patiently prowl, often stalking their prey for hours. When they decide to pounce, the result is lethal. The Arabs have a saying, "The lion's den is never without bones."[1] The easiest animals to take down are sheep, which have no natural defenses. Unless a fearless and capable shepherd comes in between them, a "lion will lie down with a lamb" only for dinner.

When you think of shepherds and lions, a king-to-be from Bethlehem quickly comes into view. As a young man David had faced threats in the Wilderness of Judah with resolve and courage. His *hutzpah* to challenge Goliath came in part from personal history with menacing marauders in the wilderness: "Your servant has been keeping his father's sheep. When a lion or a bear came and carried off a sheep from the flock, I went after it, struck it and rescued the sheep from its mouth. When it turned on me, I seized it by its hair, struck it and killed it."[a] David's response to the most intimidating natural threat in his world was *to go after it*. His weapons were simple, but his confidence was rock solid. Goliath was just another arrogant lion to kill.

I discovered that lion imagery in the ancient world was often used for royal leaders in their military role. Kings from Assyria and Babylon, for example, would

a. 1 Sam. 17:34–35

depict themselves as shepherds of their own people, but lions among the nations. Assyrian King Sennacherib—who almost destroyed Judah during the days of King Hezekiah—turned against a rival kingdom nearer home: "*I raged like a lion* and gave the order to march into Babylonia against him."[2]

Jeremiah laments that God's people had become like a vulnerable flock before such impressive empires: "Israel is a scattered flock that lions have chased away. The first to devour him was the king of Assyria; the last to crush his bones was Nebuchadnezzar king of Babylon."[a] The prophet Amos pictures Israel's unsuccessful rescue from this God-orchestrated judgment: "As a shepherd saves from the lion's mouth only two leg bones or a piece of an ear, so will the Israelites be saved."[b]

Like these ferocious historical empires, the Bible describes other lion-like enemies who assault God's people. In alarm, the psalmist cries, "O LORD my God, I take refuge in you; save and deliver me from all who pursue me, or they will tear me like a lion and rip me to pieces."[c] An enemy, without cause, "lies in wait...from ambush he murders the innocent...like a lion in cover; he lies in wait to catch the helpless; he catches the helpless and drags them off...His victims are crushed, they collapse; they fall under his strength."[d]

The ultimate spiritual predator is the devil, known by name as Satan, Lucifer, and Beelzebub; and by role as the accuser, adversary, father of lies, tempter, and prince of this world.[e] The most graphic image of this figure is "a roaring lion looking for someone to devour."[f] He relentlessly returns for God's people with an unquenchable appetite, often "masquerading as an angel of light."[g] Human enemies may be unknowing instruments of the evil one, collaborating with an unseen diabolical force for the destruction of God's people.[3] Jesus said to Peter, "Get

a. Jer. 50:17 b. Amos 3:12 c. Ps. 7:1-2 d. Ps. 10:8-10 e. I Pet. 5:8; Job 1:6-7; Isa. 14:12; Matt. 12:24; John 8:44; I Thess. 3:5; John 12:31 f. I Peter 5:8 g. 2 Cor. 11:14

behind me, *Satan*."[a] The same Satan "entered" Judas's heart, compelling him to betray Jesus.[b]

But like the shepherd David, Jesus *went after* the enemy. With a holy vengeance he liberated vulnerable sheep from the clutching lion. Taking on a greater threat than Rome, he defeated legions of demons invisibly controlling people.[c] At the foot of a pagan temple overlooking the "gates of hell," Jesus declared war on this world's reigning lion.[4] There he gave Peter the keys to his heavenly kingdom,[d] authorizing his followers to preach the good news and to free those in Satan's grip. With the power of his word they would engage the enemy. His prayer for them was "not that you take them out of the world but that you protect them from the evil one."[e] The one they were to go after.

Paul knew that believers are engaged in this invisible war: "For our struggle is not against flesh and blood, but against the rulers, against the authorities, against the powers of this dark world and against the spiritual forces of evil in the heavenly realms."[f] The apostle stressed the importance of being protected by "the full armor of God" in this struggle,[g] emphasizing that the only effective weapon is "the sword of the Spirit, which is the word of God."[h]

Many of us find ourselves "bitten, stung, and attacked by everything out there." Like Job, we have felt the hot breath of our sinister adversary. Some have buckled under the deadly force of his clasp. I have seen the devil's "claw marks." Missionary friends shot or raped. Ministries that crashed and burned. Families "dismembered" by the lion of hell. Accidents that "just happened." Some only survive these encounters in pieces.

---

a. Matt. 16:23 b. John 13:2 c. Cf. Mark 5:1–20 d. Matt. 16:18–19 e. John 17:15 f. Eph. 6:12
g. Eph. 6:11, 13 h. Eph. 6:17

Many are held captive to the devil more subtly through seductive addictions: to drugs, alcohol, pornography, work, television, music, or the internet. The enemy's work is evident in the alarming rise of anorexia, bulimia, and self-mutilation in the West. Others are falling prey through the occult. Some are possessed by demons or oppressed by them in crippling ways. Still others are just as trapped in seemingly harmless forms of pleasure or patriotism—or even in religious activity. As the demonic figure Screwtape says, "One of our great allies at present is the Church itself."[5]

Are we fully cognizant of the spiritual battle that rages around us? Will we, like David, courageously rescue God's captive people from the enemy's jaws? Can we report, like David, "*I went after it*"? The "gates of hell" will not withstand the onslaught of his followers. Ironically, we go with no other weapon than God's powerful word. In our most intense encounters with the evil one, nothing else is of use.[6]

Martin Luther's hymn, *A Mighty Fortress Is Our God*, registers his sober realism regarding the devil's foul motives and formidable might:

> For still our ancient foe doth seek to work us woe;
> His craft and power are great, and, armed with cruel hate,
> On earth is not his equal.

But a subsequent verse articulates the Reformer's robust biblical optimism regarding our ancient adversary:

> And though this world with devils filled should threaten to undo us;
> We will not fear for God hath willed his truth to triumph through us;
> The prince of darkness grim; we tremble not for him;
> His rage we can endure, for lo, his doom is sure;
> *One little word shall fell him.*

For I will be like a lion to Ephraim, like a great lion to Judah.
I will tear them to pieces and go away;
I will carry them off, with no one to rescue them.

—Hosea 5:14

The Other Lion

Majestic and fierce, the Asian lion used to dominate the animal kingdom throughout the ancient Near East. Wherever lions still flourish they are the undisputed "kings of the jungle." Weighing between 200 and 500 pounds, they can take down animals much larger in size and destroy them instantly with their powerful jaws. Lions stalk in dense brush, thickets, and grasslands, waiting for the perfect moment to pounce on unsuspecting animals. Sometimes they raid another carnivore's picnic; no other animal will challenge the lion's preeminence. I vividly recall approaching a sitting lion during a trip to Africa. The sense of danger was thick in the air, and the Land Rover, all of a sudden, seemed useless protection. The infamous roar still echoes in my mind.

In our last investigation we found ancient kings comparing themselves to lions, ravaging enemy nations as helpless flocks. Israel had its Lion too. In Isaiah, God is a growling lion, "a great lion over his prey, who is not disturbed by a band of shepherds arrayed against him."[a]

---

a. Isa. 31:4

In Jeremiah's day the Divine Lion promised to wreak havoc on the shepherd leaders of Babylon, the nation that had taken advantage of God's flock:

> *Like a lion* coming up from the thickets of the Jordan against a perennial pasture, I will suddenly chase them away from her; and I will appoint over her whomever I choose. For who is like me? Who can summon me? *Who is the shepherd who can stand before me?*... Surely the little ones of the flock shall be dragged away; surely their fold shall be appalled at their fate. (Jer. 50:44–45 NRSV)

We know this regal, judging lion later in the book of Revelation. He is the Lion King of Judah who will put all of his enemies under his feet.[a]

The biblical image of God as protective lion was reassuring to those who had seen the ravaging effects of this world's lion kings. But a troubling twist to the image is present in many passages of Scripture. Hezekiah, surely one of Judah's finest kings, prays at the end of his life: "Like a shepherd's tent my house has been pulled down and taken from me...I waited patiently till dawn, *but like a lion he broke all my bones*; day and night you made an end of me."[b] Waiting for divine help, Hezekiah met a lion intent on his destruction.

It was God.

We might think Hezekiah's perspective was skewed by personal pain. But other passages in the Bible explicitly identify God behind the terrifying roar and the deadly pounce. Hosea quotes God *vowing* to "be like a lion to Ephraim, like a great lion to Judah. I will tear them to pieces and go away; I will carry them off, with no one to rescue them."[c] Yes, God was purposefully intent on destroying the people of Israel.

Somehow, we have to reckon with this disturbing view of God. The Divine Shepherd shifts from sustainer to killer: "I cared for you in the desert, in the land

---

a. Rev. 5-6 b. Isa. 38:12–13 c. Hosea 5:14 (cf. Jer. 25:30-38; Lam. 3:10-18)

of burning heat. When I fed them, they were satisfied; when they were satisfied, they became proud; then they forgot me. *So I will come upon them like a lion...*"[a]

How did God's people react when their protective Shepherd became a threatening lion? In a community lament Israel asks how long God's anger will "smolder against the prayers of your people."[b] They cannot comprehend why, "At *your* rebuke *your* people perish."[c] Their only hope is to call on the "Shepherd of Israel, you who lead Joseph like a flock."[d]

How did godly undershepherds respond when the curtain of judgment was coming down? They too pled for mercy from the One who held the power both to harm them and to save them. In certain striking cases I find them pleading for mercy from the God whose righteous judgment was imminent. Who else could they turn to?

Some of the Bible's greatest intercessors discovered this ironic dimension to their role as shepherds. They developed a fundamental understanding that *leading is interceding*. Moses, like Abraham before him, begged God not to destroy a whole community, knowing that it had become corrupt.[e] Moses' prayer reflected a complete abandonment to share their destiny: "Now, please forgive their sin—but if not, then blot me out of the book you have written."[f] God would have eliminated his flock "had not Moses, his chosen one, stood in the breach before him to keep his wrath from destroying them."[g] A breach was a break in the wall, a vulnerability, an exposure. Moses was the only protection between God's people and God's judgment. I'm taken aback by the stubborn, reckless courage of an intercessor challenging the Lion of Heaven.

Apparently God deliberately uses approaching crises to create a fierce loyalty to the flock a shepherd serves. Moses' prayers increasingly cement his resolve

a. Hosea 13:5-7 (cf. Amos 1:2) b. Ps. 80:4 c. Ps. 80:16 d. Ps. 80:1 e. Cf. Gen. 18:23-32
f. Exod. 32:32 g. Ps. 106:23

to protect Israel not only as God's people, but also as "my people."[1] The idea that God wants someone to stop the judgment is explicit in Ezekiel: "I looked for a man among them who would...stand before me in the breach on behalf of the land so I would not have to destroy it, but I found none."[a] Finding a caring and courageous intercessor was God's objective.

In an ancient rabbinic commentary God chides Noah for failing to intercede as a true pastor for his generation. "Foolish shepherd!...I lingered with you and spoke to you at length so that you would ask for mercy for the world! But...the evil of the world did not touch your heart. You built the ark and saved yourself."[2] In this fictitious dialog Noah resembles Jonah, the prophet whose heart was unaffected by the plight of the Ninevites. Impending doom for others was of no concern to God's prophet. Just let the Lion have its prey.

The author who gives us disturbing insight into the devil's work in *The Screwtape Letters* provides an unsettling view of God in *The Lion, The Witch, and The Wardrobe*. In this fictional but theologically laced novel, C. S. Lewis depicts God as a wise and majestic lion named Aslan. Among the most memorable descriptions of the royal figure is found in Mr. Beaver's answer to Susan's question, "Is he—quite safe?" The Narnian guide replied, "Who said anything about safe? 'Course he isn't safe. But he's good. He's the king, I tell you."[3]

My mind is reeling with some disquieting questions as I consider our Shepherd Lion with his treacherous behavior and his incredulous expectations. I wonder how much I've domesticated God in my mind, unwilling to imagine the King of the Universe as unsafe.

---

a. Ezek. 22:30 (author's translation)

I also wonder if the fate of my flock touches my heart enough to challenge a just sentence? Enough to risk my own destiny for just one more chance *for them*? Do I want mercy more than justice for others? Do I "stand in the breach" recklessly interceding for my flock? I cannot honestly say that my prayers are persistent even for those who are relatively innocent. I want what Paul says of Epaphras to be true of me: He is "always wrestling in prayer for you."[a]

We really have a precarious role as spiritual shepherds. We're called to protect others with passionate abandon before each of two lions: on the one hand, the roaring devil of hell who uses any means to kill and destroy, and, on the other hand, the heavenly Lion of Judah who, on occasion, requires an intercessor to keep his anger at bay. Leadership requires defying the open jaws of both.

---

a. Col. 4:12

I am the gate.

—John 10:7

Gatekeepers

One of my last and most treasured interviews was with Moshe, a seasoned Yemenite shepherd who was eighty-something (no one knew for sure). By this time my ten-year-old daughter Adrienne was fluent in Modern Hebrew and proud to be my translator. Moshe had grown up all over the Middle East, literally. He and his wife had been orphaned as children and never formally married. They just traveled and worked together in Yemen, Saudi Arabia, Egypt, and now Israel.

Moshe has never been far from flocks and now, during the final chapter of his life, he still maintains a small herd. The family ribs him about the hassle of keeping his sheep outside their *Moshav* (cooperative village), especially at his age. But he can't imagine life without them.

I ask Moshe about the challenges of shepherding here in the hill country of Israel, and he immediately laments his biggest difficulty. Adrienne double-checks some of the words he's using but manages to convey his greatest challenge. *Thieves.* Three times he has found his pens emptied by shrewd thieves who poisoned the dogs and quietly loaded dozens of his sheep into trucks. Once he had two hundred and fifty taken.

"Are you sure he said two hundred and fifty?"

He said it again, and this time I understood the number. I found it hard to imagine that many animals—so easily frightened by nature—carted off in the night without anyone hearing a sound. Adrienne and I couldn't begin to comprehend the

grief of a man whose identity was tied so thoroughly to a flock that *others keep taking.*

Moshe took us to his pen to show us the new double metal doors. A big padlock sat on the hasp on the front door. If this were broken, he had a hidden latch that could only be opened with a long pole placed in between the two doors at just the right angle. He showed us how it worked, proud of a system he believed to be thief-proof. While these mechanical devices would probably work for awhile, they weren't adequate replacements for his personal presence. With no one sleeping near the pen, the chances of another break-in were quite likely. A good shepherd has to be shrewd, but he also has to *be there.*

Along with the animal marauders in the wilderness, shepherds have constantly had to face members of their own species stealing their flocks. For centuries, raids have been the preferred means to accumulate mobile wealth,[1] sometimes called the "bank account on hooves." Over one hundred thousand sheep were stolen in Sardinia during a nine-year period.[2] Sheep thievery is still a global phenomenon, and in some places it is an initiation rite for young men. Occasionally a thief will literally dress in sheep's wool as a disguise.[3]

Shepherds team up with guard dogs to make sure that no stranger is prowling around their herds. At night a group of herders will resort to caves or walled enclosures where they "fold" their flocks, counting them out one-by-one. A traditional stone pen includes walls on which the shepherd might place brambles and loose stones. The sound of rustling brambles and tumbling stones is the alarm that signals an intruder.

In Bible times a shepherd would sleep in the opening of a desert pen to personally guard the only access to his precious livestock. With this cultural context in mind, Jesus could as easily say, "I am the gate" as "I am the Good Shepherd."[a] As a symbolic gate, the shepherd was the only means by which someone could have access to the fold. Jesus said, "The man who does not enter the sheep pen by the gate, but climbs in by some other way, is a thief and a robber."[b] Only when the shepherd moves, do the sheep move out in safety.[c]

a. John 10:7, 9, 11 b. John 10:1 c. John 10:1-5

As we've already discovered, this parable was indirectly labeling the religious leaders of Jesus' day as thieves and robbers. The Good Shepherd's angry accusation was fully justified because God's valued flock had been carted off in the night by those put in charge of guarding them!

One of the great ironies in the world of shepherds—whether literal or figurative—is that the best thieves are good shepherds. Not good in the sense that Jesus was. But extraordinarily effective in gaining a following.

Having worked in a number of institutional settings, I appreciate the importance of a comprehensively secure environment. We need fences, locks, alarm systems, security guards, and safety lights. Our computers require constantly updated virus protection and filters for invasive spyware. We purchase insurance policies. All of this effort, technology, and expense provides a substantial measure of physical security, safety, and protection. However, I've also come to realize that human beings are vulnerable in countless ways to invisible forces and threats. Jesus was referring to spiritual thieves in his Good Shepherd parable. Spiritual safety can't be maintained without spiritual gatekeepers who spend time carefully listening for sounds of treachery.

How might we better secure the "pens" where our flocks come each day? Perhaps we need to update some systems and policies. But do we as leaders also need to be physically present more often so that the flock can better discern the voices of strangers?

On a spiritual level, do we need to increase our corporate prayer? Not just agenda-driven intercession, but open-ended listening prayer.

Our dean of students begins her daily work by praying regularly through the school's student directory. She asks the Lord to show her who needs spiritual protection through prayer and who might need personal intervention. Over the years God has brought to her attention countless sheep who were at risk of being stolen. The "thieves" might be abusive spouses, cultic religious leaders, or popular voices for immoral behavior. This dean is a spiritual gatekeeper with a keen ear for tumbling stones.

Israel's watchmen are blind, they all lack knowledge;
they are all mute dogs, they cannot bark.

—Isaiah 56:10

Dogs

That day in June wasn't the first time we were confronted with angry dogs. I'm not sure if I can remember a flock that *didn't* have barking guards come out to challenge us. However, when we approached the camp of some Beni Khalid Bedouin, their dogs wouldn't stop. We tried to signal to the shepherds in the tent that we wanted to talk, but they didn't call off the dogs. Obviously they had no interest in an interview that day.

On most occasions the dogs we encountered were given a signal that the strangers were to be treated as guests. On the shepherd's command we could pass the bared teeth and mingle with the family and flock. Still, we never felt totally unaware of the untrusting canines. Their instinct was *not* to trust.

For many predators, a herder's dogs are their biggest challenge. Dogs willingly sacrifice their lives in a nighttime brawl with their stronger cousins, the wolves. Unless thieves are prepared to kill the dogs somehow, they won't find access to a flock even in a wide-open plain. Thieves do poison dogs, but chances are the canine guards will bark before they give up their lives.

Though sheepdogs are the sheep's most loyal four-footed friends, you can tell that they are not popular among the herds. Dogs incessantly bark, bare their fangs, and exhibit an unsettling capacity for aggressive behavior. Ironically, they are very much like their relatives, the wolves. But their focused intent is to guard, and for this reason a flock is only well-protected when surrounded by dogs.

While these interviewing incidents indelibly imprinted the primary function of *guard* dogs in my mind, I noticed another vital role for them. The routine responsibility for herding dogs is *keeping the flock together*. I retain vivid mental images of huge flocks moving back to the tents at the end of the day, led in front by a shepherd only occasionally looking back. His confidence is partially grounded in the loyalty of a group of dogs who tirelessly circle the flock to keep any from straying. They form a mobile ring of security.

Though sheepdogs in modern times have become quintessential icons of intelligent support for shepherds, a little research reveals that dogs were not highly thought of in the world of the Bible. Most scriptural references are to undomesticated, howling and prowling scavengers. Their unclean habits included eating their own vomit and licking the sores of the sick and the corpses of the dead.[a] I discovered that other ancient cultures involved dogs in cultic practice, a fact that would only give more reason for disgust in ancient Israel.

To be called a dog was an insult.[1] By the time of the New Testament, Jews regularly used this designation for Gentiles.[b] Paul used the term ironically for *Judaizers*—Jews who preyed on believing Gentiles, trying to force them under Jewish law. The apostle explains to the Philippians that his warnings about these dogs are for the church's security: "It is a safeguard for you."[c]

I only found two references to dogs in the Bible that are potentially positive, both in shepherding contexts.[2] The first is to sheepdogs who guarded Job's flocks.[d] A Hittite law from the sixteenth century BC suggests that involving dogs in herding was, in fact, an ancient practice.[3]

The other reference is Isaiah's description at the beginning of this day's reflection. Israel's watchmen are "all mute dogs that cannot bark."[e] While the prophet's condemnation of a particular generation of leaders is negative, he presumes a positive role for spiritual

a. Ps. 59:14-15; Prov. 26:11; 2 Pet. 2:22; 1 Kgs. 21:19, 23; Luke 16:21 b. Mark 7:27
c. Phil. 3:2 (cf. 2 Pet. 2:22) d. Job 30:1 (cf. Judith 11:19 NRSV) e. Isa. 56:10

watchdogs. Perhaps Isaiah had in mind the ruling elite here, but the metaphor of a guard is especially suited to prophets. Ezekiel, for example, was appointed explicitly as a "watchman for the house of Israel."[a] Prophets were heralds of coming judgment, sounding an alarm when the community drifted from its covenant obligations. They "barked" when they sensed danger. Though typically unpopular, prophets told the truth about the present and the future. In contrast, false prophets were more interested in popularity and superficial peacekeeping. They slept while danger approached.

A decorated Vietnam veteran once said, "Most of the people in our society are sheep. They are kind, gentle, productive creatures who can only hurt one another by accident." The old war hero continued, "Then there are the wolves, and the wolves feed on the sheep without mercy." He considered himself among a third group he named the sheepdogs. "I live to protect the flock and confront the wolf."[4] He was challenging sheep—people who live in denial about wolves—to become sheepdogs when necessary.

I've reflected often about the marginal role of prophetic watchdogs, perhaps because I've found myself sounding a continuous warning that others decided was misplaced. They saw peace and I saw trouble. But I've also ignored dogs whose warnings were grounded in irrefutable facts; the truth was just too inconvenient. God gifts the church with prophets who "see what's coming," but I'm afraid the majority of us resist the caution and tire of the incessant yapping. History has exposed a church slow in responding to warnings about racism and materialism, to name just two threats. Prophets such as Martin Luther King Jr. have been killed because they were making too much noise. Because they were making too much *sense*.

---

a. Ezek. 3:17

Has God called us to make noise about a specific issue? Has our intensity waned because of a growing reputation that we bark too much? The destiny of a prophet is to sound the alarm when necessary, and for as long as necessary. Often alone.

The sheepdog is a reminder that the motive behind our daily circling is to keep the flock together. If we have become cynical nags, then perhaps our critics are right: we just bark too much. But if we are sincerely passionate about the unity of the flock, we must keep circling. The community cannot be left with mute guard dogs who cannot bark.

*He will put the sheep on his right
and the goats on his left.*

—Matthew 25:33

Justice

Shepherds will tell you that there is a "pecking order" in a flock, perhaps better thought of as a "butting order." Any herd has conflict and rivalry, expressed by frequent shoving and butting heads. Males especially can injure each other when they want to be first among equals in status, or when they simply want to be first in line for supper.

At sunset in many Bedouin camps I've witnessed a common chaotic scene. The flock returns from the fields in a cloud of dust that ascends and dissipates into the golden sky. They're headed back to receive their final supplemental feeding. The shepherds have already pumped water from trucks into open metal containers and put grain in separate feeding areas. The anxious animals, eyeing the feeding troughs, are held back until the signal is given. Then, in staggered groups, they rush to their final meal. The groupings reflect the shepherds' separation of sheep from goats and males from females, with preference given to the nursing ewes, the young, and the sick. To leave them all together would invite abuse.

Separation is the key to equity, a daily expression of pastoral justice.

In Ezekiel 34 God promised to come and rescue a scattered flock (in exile) that had been abused by self-serving shepherds, and personally to shepherd them again.[a] In this passage there are beautiful images of the Divine Shepherd compassionately regathering his flock. However, in a surprising mix of sentiments, God vows to divide them too.

> I will search for the lost and bring back the strays. I will bind up the injured and strengthen the weak, but the sleek and the strong I will destroy. I will shepherd the flock with justice. As for you, my flock, this is what the Sovereign LORD says: I will judge between one sheep and another, and between rams and goats...See, I myself will judge between the fat sheep and the lean sheep. Because you shove with flank and shoulder, butting all the weak sheep with your horns until you have driven them away, I will save my flock...I will judge between one sheep and another. (Ezek. 34:16–22)

Israel's Shepherd was coming not only to save them from their enemies, but also from themselves! He would *judge* "the sleek and the strong," "between one sheep and another," "between rams and goats," "between the fat sheep and the lean sheep." The aggressive behavior exhibited by those who were physically stronger required a referee. "Shoving" and "butting" creates an unsafe environment for those unable to defend themselves. As a responsible shepherd God would take as many precautions

a. Ezek. 34:11ff.

to protect his animals from each other as from the predators that lurked outside the fold. This Shepherd understands the power differential in the flock.

The phrase in Ezekiel that marks the shift in God's pastoral behavior makes explicit his central concern: "I will shepherd the flock *with justice.*" This dimension of leadership was widely acclaimed in the ancient world. Monarchs presented themselves publicly as generous providers and capable protectors. Their "protective spirit"[1] was expressed by defending the homeland against enemy armies. But protective leadership was exercised as often by the implementation of wise and just laws for the citizenry. Law collections became monuments to the quality of society that kings created by their rules. As a "just shepherd" King Hammurabi claimed to be a divinely-appointed shepherd ruler whose role was *"to cause justice to prevail in the land, to destroy the wicked and the evil, that the strong might not oppress the weak."*[2]

In the final Judgment Day our Divine Shepherd Judge will separate everyone into two groups. "When the Son of Man comes in his glory, and all the angels with him, he will sit on his throne in heavenly glory. All the nations will be gathered before him, and he will separate the people one from another as a shepherd separates the sheep from the goats. He will put the sheep on his right and the goats on his left."[a] What distinguishes these two groups is their treatment of "the least of these brothers of mine."[b] True to their independent nature, the "goats" are those who have shown no compassion or mercy to others. They have used their strength and independence only to serve themselves. The "sheep," known for their responsive temperaments, have been kind and merciful to the marginalized—the poor, the naked, the imprisoned, the stranger, the hungry, and the sick. The Shepherd so fully

---

a. Matt. 25:31–33 b. Vs. 40

identifies with these members of his flock that he says, "I tell you the truth, whatever you did for one of the least of these brothers of mine, *you did for me.*"[a]

One of the most precious memories in my life took place in India in 1986. My wife and I were at the Home of the Destitute and Dying in Calcutta, India, waiting to see Mother Theresa for volunteer job assignments. In front of us were rows of sick people on simple green cots—"the poorest of the poor" in the simple nun's famous words. Many had been picked up in the gutters of Calcutta's streets by the Sisters of Charity. Clothed in their simple white saris with the distinctive blue trim, the Sisters are the angels of mercy who care for Jesus, wherever they find him.

While we were waiting, I couldn't help but notice a man, weighing no more than seventy pounds, gasping for air right in front of me. One of the Sisters came to his side and gently propped up his head in her hand. She carefully brought a dented metal cup to his lips and helped him swallow a little water. All I could think of was Jesus' words, "when you saw me thirsty, you gave me to drink."

The next morning at the 6:00 AM mass we saw a crucifix above the altar with the words, "I thirst; We quench." The words of Jesus in Matthew 25 formed the vision for this ministry, shaping the identity of a whole community of servants.

But Mother Theresa was known for more than ministries of compassion. She once said, "When I helped the poor, I was called a saint. But when I asked *why* they were poor, I was called a communist." She knew that compassion ultimately leads to justice. She called on those in positions of power to use it for the marginalized. True concern goes to the root. We become advocates. We look for systemic causes. We speak up for the "little ones." We fight for justice. One of the

a. Vs. 40

Proverbs reads, "Speak up for those who cannot speak for themselves...defend the rights of the poor and needy."[a]

As we reflect on these themes in the context of our ministries, consider how compassion leads to justice. Have some begun a ministry with the sick and then found themselves dealing with careless hospital help or insurance disputes over medication? Has work with the homeless led someone into job training and placement programs? Has protest against abortion led to involvement in a crisis pregnancy center? Shepherd leaders have an eye for equity. Shepherd leaders look for opportunities to enfranchise the disenfranchised. We feel compelled to move from individual need to institutional cause. We build and enforce boundaries that protect those who are "lean" and defenseless. Because Jesus is among them.

---

a. Prov. 31:8–9

Shepherd your people with your rod.

—Micah 7:14

The Rod

Ω I've never seen a shepherd with a traditional rod in the Middle East, but its use is legendary. Along with the staff, ancient shepherds carried a club, usually referred to as a rod. Typically half the size of a staff, the rod was often made from the root of a tree with a natural bulb on one end. The shepherd could tuck this versatile weapon in his belt and use it for defense against both animal and human predators. David may have killed lions and bears with his club. Today's Bedouin have traded in their rods for guns, but shepherds in parts of Africa can still throw one with deadly accuracy.

The rod has another use that is also defensive. In traditional settings the animals are counted and inspected every night as they "pass under the rod" of the shepherd.[a] Running the implement against the wool, they examine each animal for evidence of little enemies such as ticks and parasites.

Shepherds have yet another use for the rod among their flocks. Once in awhile, a shepherd might "remind" straying animals with his wooden missile that their behavior is unacceptable. This important disciplinary function of the rod ensures the flock's safety and well-being.

a. Jer. 33:13; Ezek. 20:37

Because the shepherd was such a common icon for leadership in antiquity, the rod and staff became symbols of political authority.[a] God mocked the might of Philistia when an Israelite shepherd boy confronted Goliath with herding implements. In response the giant roared, "Am I a dog that you come at me with *sticks*?"[b] Like Moses, David knew that his "sticks" had power because they represented the timely judgment of God.

Once I recognized the rod's different forms I discovered a widespread tendency to associate it with royal rule and military might. The rod became stylized in the court, taking the form of a scepter. For example, in Psalm 2:9 there is a prediction that the Messiah will shepherd the nations with an iron rod, smashing them like pottery.[1] Many translations understandably use the term *scepter*, though an ancient audience would have understood the pastoral symbolism.

In royal documents from Mesopotamia and Egypt, I found the scepter equated not only with power but also with orderly rule. Power with respect to outsiders; order with respect to the kingdom. Assyrian King Tikulti Ninurta I called himself "the true shepherd who through the justice of his scepter keeps people and communities in order."[2] The same sentiment is found in Scripture: "Your royal scepter is a scepter of equity; you love righteousness and hate wickedness."[c] A sizeable current in ancient literature associates strong *pastoral* leadership with a rod of order and equity.

Psalm 2:9 isn't the only passage that depicts a coming Messiah who would bring a just and safe order by the emblem of his ruling rod. The prophet Isaiah paints a beatific vision of paradise preceded by the use of Messiah's rod:

> With righteousness he will judge the needy, with justice he will give decisions for the poor of the earth. *He will strike the earth with the*

---

a. Gen 49:10; Num 21:8; Ezek 19:11, 14. b. 1 Sam. 17:43 c. Ps. 45:6–7 (cf. Heb. 1:8)

rod of his mouth; with the breath of his lips he will slay the wicked. Righteousness will be his belt and faithfulness the sash around his waist. The wolf will live with the lamb, the leopard will lie down with the goat, the calf and the lion and the yearling together. (Isa. 11:4–6)

The Messianic era is possible because of a fundamental principle understood in antiquity: Protection and discipline breed security. The psalmist reflects this dynamic with poetic simplicity when he says, "Your rod and staff, they comfort me."[a]

The emblem of militant protection is the same rod used for discipline. In Psalm 89:32 God promised to punish Israel's sin with a rod. The book of Proverbs applies the principle to sound parenting: "Those who spare the rod hate their children, but those who love them are diligent to discipline them."[b] God is the Heavenly Parent who loves his children by disciplining them.[c]

New Testament accounts of church discipline reveal the same radical concern for order

photo courtesy of Dr. James C. Martin. The Cairo Museum
a. Ps. 23:4 b. Prov. 13:24 (NRSV) c. Prov. 3:11–12; Heb. 12:5–7

and righteousness. Peter confronted Ananias and Sapphira for a monetary gift that was less than promised. God confirmed Peter's assessment with their immediate deaths.[a] Paul called for judgment on those who had abandoned their conscience and shipwrecked their faith: "Among them are Hymenaeus and Alexander, whom I have handed over to Satan to be taught not to blaspheme."[b]

In most cases discipline is separating someone from the flock. "Have nothing to do with them!"[c] Paul says to Timothy, speaking of those with false spirituality. The apostle's advice to Titus regarding troublemakers was, "Warn a divisive person once, and then warn him a second time. After that, have nothing to do with him."[d]

Security and comfort are the fruits of shepherd leaders who exercise judgment and discipline. But not everyone in leadership accepts this kind of work. Some parents design a "good cop/bad cop" arrangement with their children with threats like, "Just wait till your father gets home!" Some pastors, afraid or tired of maintaining order and discipline, use an associate or outside firm to do the "dirty work." The shepherds I met in the field wouldn't have understood this dichotomization. Creating and enforcing rules is *pastoral* ministry. Confronting and removing abusive members from a congregation is as much shepherding as nurturing young and needy ones. Shepherd leadership provides comfort not only through gentleness but also through discipline.[e] It takes both the staff and the rod to lead.

In my work with pastors I am sometimes greeted with the words, "I'm so tired of all I'm expected to do. *I just want to be a shepherd.*" Assuming that I would welcome these sentiments, most are surprised when I respond, "You've probably

a. Acts 5:1–10 b. I Tim. 1:20 c. 2 Tim. 3:5 d. Tit. 3:10 e. 2 Sam. 7:14; Prov. 13:24; Isa. 10:15

come to the wrong person." I want to make sure that pastors aren't running away from the hard tasks of leading people. I can't support the assumption that shepherding is simply about nurture and "pastoral care."

Paul sent a letter to the Corinthians encouraging them to prepare for his visit. There were cases of blatant immorality and other forms of misconduct for which the church felt no remorse. He gave them the choice of which kind of shepherd they would greet: "What do you desire? Shall I come to you with a rod, or with love and a spirit of gentleness?"[a]

Paul could go either way. Can we?

Before we leave the topic of discipline, we may need to pause and ask ourselves whether or not *we* are responsive to the rod in our lives. Sometimes our official positions of leadership excuse us from personal accountability. Of course, there are government regulations and institutional checks and balances. But civil institutions cannot be expected to reinforce discipline prescribed within a religious community.

As shepherds, we need to intentionally seek out wise and objective individuals to whom we can submit for thorough, ongoing assessment. I refer to this group of individuals in my life as my personal board of directors. Another friend calls his group his three wise men. We each have to decide who is best suited to gently interrogate us on a routine basis. Otherwise we may become too accustomed to holding the rod and lose sight of its potential liabilities.

---

a. 1 Cor. 4:21 (NASB)

The good shepherd lays down his life for the sheep.

—John 10:11

A Living Sacrifice

This time I knew I had to do it myself.

After studying animal husbandry for a year, I had witnessed the slaughter of many animals. Yet I desired a more direct and even intimate experience with the process.

Not because I enjoyed killing.

Rather, for personal and theological reasons I needed to be the one who slit the throat of a harmless, patient, perfect lamb. I had to be the one responsible for its death. We rightly say that neither Romans nor Jews killed Jesus. Instead each one of us bears the blame for putting him on the cross. We put the nails in his hands. I needed to express physically what I had done to the Lamb of God.

The occasion came in January 2007 when I was back in Israel leading a tour that featured experiential learning. One bright morning in the Jordan Valley Hazim met us outside his tent and pointed toward the two men waiting with the designated lamb. Our group watched as they turned the full-sized animal on her side and held her gently in place on the ground.

She hardly struggled.

Slaughter has to be done correctly. The cut has to be swift and final so the suffering is minimal. They gave me a knife and I briskly slid it across the sheep's neck, but the skin remained uncut.

The sheep didn't move.

I tried again. *Maybe I hadn't put enough force behind my cut.* Again, no blood. By this time our group was painfully aware of how compliant the animal was, just waiting for this amateur to cut its throat. I cried *"kharam"* to Hazim, suggesting that the slaughter had become disqualified.

Hazim urged me to try again. The lamb waited pathetically for the delayed execution. Our group shuddered as the trauma unfolded.

After a third unsuccessful attempt, Hazim examined the knife and admitted that it was dull. What agony for all of us!

Finally, after the knife was sharpened, I took the instrument and quickly slit the still passive lamb's throat.

There was a great deal of sobbing as crimson poured across the ashen gravel. The lamb's liquid life emptied in seconds while the body quivered. It was difficult to watch, but I had insisted. After some emotionally charged moments of silence, I managed to read a portion of Isaiah 53 and then with tears we sang a song about the saving blood of Jesus:

> There is a fountain filled with blood drawn from Immanuel's veins;
> And sinners plunged beneath that flood lose all their guilty stains.
> Dear dying Lamb, thy precious blood shall never lose its power
> Till all the ransomed church of God be saved to sin no more.
> Ever since by faith I saw the stream thy flowing wounds supply,
> Redeeming love has been my theme, and shall be till I die.[1]

Perhaps the most disturbing element of the parable in John 10 is the central place of sacrifice. The greatest act of the Good Shepherd—the one that brought to culmination his life of service—was submitting like a lamb to slaughter. The Good Shepherd was, all along, the Lamb of God. Jesus had said in Matthew to "go to the lost sheep of Israel," highlighting the disciples' role as assistant *shepherds* in his pastoral ministry. But, in that same commission, he tells them that they were going as "*sheep* among wolves."[a] Like the Chief Shepherd, they were going defenselessly, without protection, like sheep to their own deaths.

Jesus told Peter three times to demonstrate his love for the Lord by feeding and shepherding his sheep. He then immediately indicated that Peter would follow Jesus in death.[b] In his kingdom, *leading means bleeding.*[2] "If any want to become my followers...let them take up their cross."[c] The One who will be worshipped in heaven forever, according to Revelation 5, is an ironic mix of Ruling Lion and Slain Lamb.

The destitution and deaths of early martyrs are celebrated marks of their honorable faith in Hebrews 11: "They were stoned; they were sawed in two; they were

a. Matt. 10:6, 16 b. John 21:15–19 c. Mark 8:34 (NRSV)

put to death by the sword. They went about in sheepskins and goatskins, destitute, persecuted and mistreated." Then follows that most memorable line: "*the world was not worthy of them.*"[a]

Most leaders in Scripture found their calling to be a *living* sacrifice.[b] While Paul's ministry put him in constant danger of physical death,[c] he says in 1 Corinthians 15:31, "I die every day!"[d] He saw his life being poured out like a sacrificial offering for those he loved.[e] He understood the psalmist's words, "Precious in the sight of the Lord is the death of his saints."[f]

The unforgettable image from that morning in the Jordan Valley reminds me of Reverend Josef Ton, a leader of the persecuted church in Romania. He had once shaken my world as a seminary student with his simple, firmly-held conviction that martyrdom was essential to Christian discipleship. He had faced death willingly on many occasions. In one of his books he writes:

> What made me able to face this possibility with peace and joy was the understanding that martyrdom is a very essential part of the way God chooses to tackle the evil of this world. Suffering and

---

a. Heb. 11:37–38 b. Rom. 12:1 c. 2 Cor. 11:23 d. (NRSV) e. Phil. 2:17 f. Ps. 116:15

self-sacrifice are, first of all, God's selected methods for his own involvement in history and for the accomplishment of his purposes with mankind. When he chooses human instruments, therefore, to achieve his purposes through them, God uses the same methods he employed with his Son.[3]

Since the first century a steady stream of blood has spilled for the cause of Christ. Over one hundred million Christians have given the ultimate witness within the last century alone.[4] This sacrifice has served to spread the gospel. "The blood of the martyrs," said early church leader Tertullian, "is the seed of the church."[5]

For most of us the call to serve sacrificially requires a different kind of ongoing fatality. To give life to others, we give of our own life. We catch glimpses of what Paul meant when he said, "Death is at work in us, but life in you."[a] Pastoral work requires dying to ambition and comfort and every other self-centered craving— for others. It means "spending and being spent"[b] and "seeking the interests of others above our own."[c] Whether in physical death or as a "living sacrifice," we are called to death. Only in that death is resurrection life available to others.

How do we lay down our lives for our sheep? In what ways do we "die every day" for our members, our staff, our children? Would the death of certain attitudes, habits, or possessions enable us to serve more freely? Do we need to pray for faith to submit to the knife and let go of our lives?

A blood-stained sheepskin hangs in my office to remind me of what I did to the Lamb of God and what the Lamb of God did for me—*and what the Lamb expects of me.*

---

a. 2 Cor. 4:12; 11:23-29 b. 2 Cor. 12:15 c. Phil. 2:4

The night is nearly over; the day is almost here.

—Romans 13:12

Darkness

As the molten sun descends behind the desert's desolate landscape, the daylight's eye-squinting brilliance is slowly overcome by a heavy darkness that creeps down *wadi* walls and spreads across each valley's open ground. A shepherd and flock traveling home at the end of the day are swallowed by the invading shadows. Dangers escalate in the deepening darkness. Night is the kingdom of predators.

Shepherds who move their flocks at night do so at great risk. They hope for help from the moon and stars which they study well. Under the cover of a black sky, mischief will flourish. We've observed attentive guards on alert for thieves, wild animals, and looming storms. Shepherds who lack desert-savvy easily lose all sense of orientation—and often lose their nerve.

The speeches of Job are laced with words for darkness; most of the book could be characterized as a cry in the dark. The light of his life had gone out and he groped for the God who promised to be there. In one passage alone Job uses five different terms for darkness as he considers the prospect of death: "...before I go to the place of no return, to the land of gloom and deep shadow, to the land of deepest night, of deep shadow and disorder, where even the light is like darkness."[a] In his darkest hours the patriarchal shepherd felt vulnerable before all of his foes and found no evidence of God's presence.

Darkness is the choice setting for the work of God's enemies. Job mentions thieves and evildoers who hide in the dark.[b] Sinners engage in works of darkness.[c] The devil's realm is the kingdom of darkness, and utter darkness is another name for hell.[d]

One of the many words Job uses for darkness is *tsalmavet*, found ten times throughout the book. This graphic compound term can be translated "shadow of death" or "deadly darkness." We're familiar with the phrase in The Shepherd Psalm: "Even though I walk through the valley of the *shadow of death*, I will fear no evil, for you are with me."[e] Here the psalmist is unafraid to walk through the valley of *tsalmavet* because the Lord accompanies him. This valley symbolizes life's hazardous transitions—occasions when the Shepherd Guide could be trusted without the illumination of daylight.

Tsalmavet characterized the deserts of Sinai and the Negev where Israel spent forty years. Jeremiah criticized a later generation for forgetting God's presence there: "They did not say, 'Where is the LORD who brought us up out of the land of

a. Job 10:21–22 b. Job 24:16; 34:22 c. Eph. 5:11–12 d. Col. 1:13; 2 Pet. 2:17; Jude 13 e. Ps. 23:4

Egypt, who led us through the wilderness...through a land of drought and of *deep darkness?*"[a] The unsuspecting community was about to pass into the deadly shadow of exile, a seventy-year spiritual wilderness: "Give glory to the LORD your God before he brings the darkness, before your feet stumble on the darkening hills. You hope for light, but he will turn it to *thick darkness* and change it to deep gloom."[b]

The good news for these exiles was the dawn of redemption. "He brought them out of darkness and the *deepest gloom* and broke away their chains."[c] The true light was beyond their return to Israel. Isaiah promised, "The people who walk in darkness will see a great light. The light will shine on those who live in *death's shadow.*"[d] Jesus Christ would end the community's *tsalmavet* and usher in the dawning of the Day of the Lord.

An essential metaphor for the Light of the World's ministry was giving sight to the blind.[e] He literally healed those without physical sight. But spiritual blindness was more serious; it characterized the whole community, especially the shepherd leaders.

In John 9 Jesus heals a blind man who then becomes an uninvited witness to the religious leaders. Their unresponsiveness prompts Jesus to declare *them* blind.[f] They were lost in deadly darkness. And in that condition they had become arrogant and abusive towards a man who simply responded to Jesus in faith. With this episode as a backdrop, Jesus tells the parable of the Good Shepherd in John 10. The thieves, hirelings, and wolves he mentions are these leaders. They work mischief in the darkness; they are the children of the devil.[f]

Darkness in the Bible is the devil's time when God's people and plan are put at risk. Is it any surprise that these leaders came *at night* to arrest Jesus? His explanation was incisive: "Every day I was with you in the temple courts, and

---

a. Jer. 2:6 (NASB) b. Jer. 13:16 c. Ps. 107:14 d. Isa. 9:2 (author's translation); Matt. 4:16; Luke 1:79 e. Luke 4:18 f. John 8:44

you did not lay a hand on me. *But this is your hour—when darkness reigns.*"[a] An extraordinary darkness blanketed the next afternoon as Jesus hung on the cross.[b] Like Job, Jesus experienced abandonment and utter isolation from God in his suffering.[c]

But dawn would shatter that night when hell was unleashed on the Lamb of God.

Just as God's light overpowered the darkness at Creation, so the ruler of darkness and the grip of death surrendered to the King of Light at Christ's resurrection.[d] All believers are united to Christ in his holy brilliance: "You are all children of light and children of the day; we are not of the night or of darkness."[e]

Many of us have experienced the desperate isolation and cold darkness that Job describes in his memoir. These seasons of life without the light of understanding or any sense of God's presence test our faith in an invisible Shepherd. My wife and I journeyed through such deadly shadows for several years when our children were young. Faced with disabilities and the resulting shift in our life's direction, we entered *tsalmavet*. The light we longed for did not dawn as we expected. Only slowly did we reemerge from this valley as sobered believers and humbled leaders.

When a friend recently explained the devastating impact a family tragedy was wreaking on their spiritual life, I couldn't respond like Job's friends.

I simply said, "Welcome to the darkness. There are more questions than answers in this place. But you'll find good company among those who understand how little we understand—but still hold on to God's hand."

---

a. Luke 22:53 b. Luke 23:44 c. Matt. 27:46 d. 2 Cor. 4:6 e. 1 Thess. 5:5

Saint John of the Cross describes a particular kind of spiritually arid experience as the "dark night of the soul." This journey through shadows purges the soul of its pride and earthly attachments.[2] Our challenge in dry and dark times is to respond in simple faith—to believe that the unseen Divine Shepherd is with us in our unlit valley. We grope in hope until rays of light begin to push the night away. Eventually, as Job confessed, "He reveals mysteries from the darkness, and brings the *tsalmavet* into the light."[a]

These shadows come at unplanned and awkward times in our ministries as leaders. Just when we need to show enthusiasm for a vision. Just when our families need us most. Just when we thought we could enjoy the status quo. When we least expect it, the lights go out. And our faith, the only fire in the soul's night, barely smolders.

As we remember those segments of our journey that have been covered in deep shadows, can we now see some evidence of the Shepherd's presence? If not, will we continue to walk by faith and not by sight?[b] How do we respond to others who feel destabilized in a dark spiritual wilderness? Do we try to fix their feelings with pat answers, or are we content to sit with them in *tsalmavet*?

If the darkness has settled across our employees, have we looked for ways to replace them with happier or more productive individuals, or have we treasured them as uniquely vulnerable to the deep work of God?

Having emerged from some dark valleys, do we now have a more balanced response to the "mountain tops"? Are we ready for more valleys, should they come—even the "valley of the shadow of death"?

---

a. Job 12:22 (NASB) b. 2 Cor. 5:7

Be on guard for yourselves.

—Acts 20:28

Guard Yourselves

We have reflected awhile on the shepherd's role as guard and watchman. Especially at night, the herders are the only protection that defenseless sheep have from wolves and thieves. But what happens when guards conspire against the owner who hires them? What if their secret intention is stealing the sheep? This can happen. The bonding and loyalty that develops between a flock and the one who spends the most time with them can create a temptation to walk away with them. When the guard becomes the enemy, the flock is in deep trouble.

I was surprised to find a current of antagonism and mistrust between owners and non-family hired help. Field hands are often seasonal workers who feel disinclined to sacrifice too much for a job with high demand, limited benefits, and no long-term commitment. "The employer, on the other hand, fears animal loss and injury and suspects that the shepherd, once away from the tent and out of sight, ignores the flock and sleeps in the sun. Employers often complain that shepherds care nothing about hard work or correct techniques of animal husbandry."[1] Ever since ancient times it has been "a common belief among herd owners that shepherds will steal or eat their sheep if given a chance. They demand to see the skin of each sheep that dies or is slaughtered to assure themselves that their livestock is not being sold."[2]

When I turned to Scripture I noticed the same feelings of suspicion in the stories of Laban and Jacob. Though Jacob was both nephew and son-in-law, he felt so mistrusted that he ran away from his uncle in Paddan-aram to preserve the holdings that were rightfully his. When Laban caught up with him, Jacob explained: "I have been with you for twenty years now. Your sheep and goats have not miscarried, nor have I eaten rams from your flocks. I did not bring you animals torn by wild beasts; I bore the loss myself. And you demanded payment from me for whatever was stolen by day or night."[a]

Unlike Jacob, many shepherds in biblical times could not be trusted to guard an owner's flock.[b] Not only field hands but spiritual shepherds too. While the Bible clearly teaches that "the laborer deserves to be paid,"[c] there is a consistent criticism of those who see God's work simply as a means to serve their own appetites. Ezekiel cries, "Woe to the shepherds of Israel who only take care of themselves! Should not shepherds take care of the flock? You eat the curds, clothe yourselves with the wool and slaughter the choice animals, but you do not take care of the flock."[d] The community was being "fleeced" by leaders commissioned to care for them.[3] In so doing these non-shepherds became allies of the predators from whom they were called to guard the flock! "So they were scattered because there was no shepherd, and when they were scattered *they became food for all the wild animals.*"[e]

In his warning to the Ephesian elders, Paul carries Ezekiel's thought to its logical conclusion. We considered this passage earlier regarding external threats in

a. Gen. 31:38–39 b. Jn 10:13 c. 1 Tim. 5:18 (NRSV) d. Ezek. 34:2–3 (cf. Jude 12) e. Ezek. 34:5

Ephesus. Their church planter now makes the alarming prediction that many who were currently faithful guardians would *turn into wolves*.

> *Be on guard for yourselves* and for all the flock, among which the Holy Spirit has made you overseers, to shepherd the church of God which He purchased with His own blood. I know that after my departure savage wolves will come in among you, not sparing the flock; and *from among your own selves* men will arise, speaking perverse things, to draw away the disciples after them. *Therefore be on the alert.* (Acts 20:28–31, NASB)

Some of *you*, he says, will become the enemy. *You* will take the flock away from the very Owner who hired you.

For Paul, guardians become wolves or false-shepherds not only when they fleece the flock, but also when they lure God's people away by false teaching. As effective communicators, counterfeit teachers provide attractive, persuasive doctrine that "looks" and "smells" like biblical truth, but their teaching is subtly divisive and ultimately destructive. While some gain a following by catering to "itching ears," others evidence a need to cause division.[a] Sheep that thrive on controversy and confusion willingly follow a guard-turned-wolf.

These passages force me to ask questions about my own motives. *Do I exist to serve the sheep and their Shepherd, or do they exist to serve me?* One of the common criticisms of hired shepherds is that they are "only in it for the money." Is ministry primarily a means to make ends meet or to make wealth? I think about Paul's choice to be self-supporting, not a "peddler" of the gospel.[b] He wanted to remove doubt in anyone's mind—maybe even his own?—that ministry was his gift to others.[c]

I wonder about my own orthodoxy too. Is my thinking comprehensively tethered to God's revealed truth or am I overly influenced by trends in popular thought? Am I grounded in God's word or captivated by compelling "original" ideas? Do I get more pleasure out of reinforcing historically orthodox truths or destabilizing a student's current belief system? Becoming a wolf only takes a combination of skepticism and time. Values shift almost imperceptibly, and new frames of reference take root. I've seen it happen too many times.

Unfortunately, good shepherds sometimes become wolves without realizing their own transformation. They become captive to ideas that they once resisted, but now promulgate. Their enhanced spiritual enlightenment is often accompanied by a "false humility."[d] One minister lost his nerve to speak of heaven and hell to those who were dying. He admitted to my wife that he was accommodating them with "whatever they needed to hear." That kind of "pastoral care," devoid of truth, paves the way to destruction.

a. 2 Tim. 4:2–4; 1 Tim. 1:2–7; 6:3–5 b. 2 Cor. 2:17 c. 2 Cor. 11:7–15 d. Col. 2:18–23

We served a short term in the Philippines with a church whose young pastor was a vocal proponent of a "health and wealth gospel." When he became ill one night, he ordered an ambulance to come secretly to his back door. This pastor didn't want anyone in his congregation to know that his theological formula wasn't working for him. His false teaching had created a large following and a substantial income. The shepherd had become a wolf.

I also know some good shepherds who have just gotten too tired to "fight the good fight of the faith."[a] Our determination to see people as God sees them is forgotten in the fatigue of important but draining ministry. We loose our theological moorings. Our identity as shepherds dissolves. The shadow of cynicism creeps into our once-tender hearts. We forget the Proverb, "Above all else, guard your heart."[b]

We've already seen that recognizing the wolves "out there" is a serious and ongoing challenge. Yet sober self-scrutiny regarding the *inner*-wolf requires even more vigilance. Who can accurately assess the urges prowling in the darkness of our own souls? We all need accountability before others who can freely "check under the wool" and see what is really there.

James understood the precariousness of being in leadership when he warned, "Not many of you should presume to be teachers, my brothers."[c] We all need to be on guard for ourselves!

---

a. 1 Tim. 6:12 b. Prov. 4:23 c. James 3:1

*He who watches over Israel will
neither slumber nor sleep.*

—Psalm 121:4

My Sleepless Shepherd

♌ Anwar was a fiercely independent young Syrian shepherd who labored for various herd owners until he got fed up with the working conditions. He would then leave with his few belongings on his horse for another job. Hired shepherds get no time off, he told me. They work every day, every night, without a break. The owners bring them food in the morning and evening, inquire about the flocks, and then leave them with their work.

I asked Anwar how long he had ever worked for an employer. "Eighteen months," he replied. Like the herders of first century Bethlehem, many Middle Eastern shepherds today are "living out in the fields...keeping watch over their flocks at night."[a] I thought of Jacob who reminded Laban that caring for his flocks was a wearisome responsibility: "This was my situation: The heat consumed me in the daytime and the cold at night, and sleep fled from my eyes."[b] An old Sumerian proverb avers, "The herdsman in his weariness cannot recognize his own mother."[1]

---

a. Luke 2:8 b. Gen. 31:40

Not all hired hands are as responsible as Jacob was. Bedouin tell stories of workers who become careless, especially when long hot days follow a succession of sleepless nights. One shepherd confessed that his owner almost killed him for carelessness: "It was in summer and I fell asleep. When I woke up the sheep had wandered off and eight were dead. The hyenas got them."[2] It's easy to fall asleep. But sleep has deadly consequences. They say a good shepherd sleeps, like a panther, with one eye open.

Anwar was probably exaggerating about his lack of support. Most herd owners I met were involved in managing the flock, though sometimes at a distance. Good owners certainly make sure that their help is given adequate time to rest. Sometimes the field help just need to trust that they're not alone.

There's no doubt that Scripture puts a high premium on hard work. A common sentiment is found in the Proverb, "One who is slack in his work is brother to one who destroys."[a] Paul said, "Respect those who work hard among you," but, "Anyone unwilling to work should not eat."[b] Too often the people of God have languished for lack of hard-working leaders. Isaiah lamented that their "watchmen are blind...they lie around and dream, *they love to sleep.*"[c]

While sluggards had no part in shepherding God's people, I discovered in Scripture a good reason for shepherds to sleep. Sometimes slumber reflects trust in the sleepless Owner's involvement. Jacob could say at the end of his journey, "God has been *my shepherd* all my life to this day."[d] The psalmist asks, "Where does my help come from? My help comes from *the LORD...he* will watch over your life; *the LORD* will watch over your coming and going both now and forevermore....*He who watches over Israel will neither slumber nor sleep.*"[e]

a. Prov. 18:9 b. 1 Thess. 5:12; 2 Thess. 3:10 (NRSV) c. Isa. 56:10 (cf. Nah. 3:18) d. Gen. 48:15
e. Ps. 121

Sleeping as an expression of faith is encouraged in Psalm 127:1-2:

Unless the LORD watches over the city the watchmen stand in vain.
In vain you rise early and stay up late, toiling for food to eat—*for
he grants sleep to those he loves.*

Conscientious leaders with a strong work ethic had to understand that they were not ultimately responsible for the welfare of their flocks. Only the Shepherd of Israel could be counted on to shoulder the full "24/7" burden of responsibility. Apparently human leaders can assume too much control over their work. The safety of God's flock is ultimately assured by *God's* unwavering vigilance always to keep one eye open.

 A friend of mine asked the pastor of a large church to disclose his "secret" for the congregation's phenomenal growth. Checking melodramatically to make sure that no one else was listening, he whispered, "Hard work!" He was being facetious because the question presumed that some little-known mystery was the

key to his leadership. But the inescapable truism of leadership is that it is round-the-clock hard work. Being in charge frequently requires being at more meetings and events, reading more reports, and listening to more stories (and all sides of each story) than others have to. We are often the ones who turn out the lights and lock the doors. We find emergency messages that call us back out after we thought the day was over. Like Jacob we yearn for the sleep that flees our eyes.

But more than the quantity of physical activity, the real weight of leadership is emotional. The greatest stress on our well-being (and our family life) is the energy required to care for a community. We can't be caught "asleep at the switch" when the flock needs us most. The constant preoccupation with *their* needs and the threats to *their* welfare leaves a shepherd feeling drained. Though we may delegate effectively to trusted associates, *we alone feel the final responsibility* for the health and success of our church or organization They have our cell phone number. They've been told how to reach us if they need to. When we are not sleepless from the physical fatigue, we frequently face restless nights with preoccupations that accompany this sense of responsibility. Even if the flock in mind is our own family, we cannot begin to weigh the burden of concern. It never ends.

The only true consolation for the relentless burden of leadership is the reality that God, the ultimate Shepherd of the flock, "neither slumbers nor sleeps." God is *already* committed to ceaseless supervision of our communities, because the people we care for are *his*. "It is *he* who made us, and we are *his*; we are *his* people, the sheep of *his* pasture."[a] God's ultimate ownership puts us in the *assistant's* role as *deputy* leaders, *associate* pastors, and *under*shepherds. We cannot bear the burden of leadership without realizing that God is the ultimate Owner of the flock. Whatever our context of ministry, we must tap into this reality to find relief during the watches of the night. "He gives sleep to those he loves."[b]

I'm left wondering, *Do I carry the burden of responsibility as though it were exclusively mine to bear, or do I trust the Owner of the flock to cover the night shift?*

At the end of the day, *leading means letting go.*

---

a. Ps. 100:3 b. Ps. 127:2

GUIDANCE

In your strength you will guide
them to your holy pasture.

—Exodus 15:13

GUIDANCE

In this last segment of our journey we'll spend some days reflecting on the guiding role of shepherd leaders. Beyond provision and protection, where are shepherds trying to take their flocks? What will it take to get there? A shepherd's guidance involves shaping mission, casting vision, and managing objectives in a constantly changing environment.

For the flock to move ahead toward the shepherd's goals of productivity and reproduction, we'll see the need for the shepherding traits of hard work, trustworthiness, adaptability, persistence, and wisdom. Sheep don't see the big picture and occasionally need to be driven to their destination.

The experience of a shepherd named Husein reminds me of the often unanticipated crises and threatening predicaments that have to be handled deftly out in the wilderness:

> Husein shouted that a storm was coming and they should move the flock back toward the tents. The herd was turned around and began moving quickly. But the large brown ewe now seemed to be in labor and could not keep up with them, and Husein had to slow up the sheep in the front. As they advanced, the ewe seemed to be experiencing more and more difficulty; she would move a few

paces, fall exhausted to the earth, rest a few moments and struggle to her feet and try to catch up...As the lightning came the ewe was giving birth...Husein jumped up and ran to assist the delivery, gently pulling the lamb from the womb...[he] gave it to the ewe to lick clean, and then he wrapped the lamb inside the folds of his cloak, tucking it carefully into the dry warmth to keep it from getting a chill.[1]

Husein was a good shepherd who could discern changes in the environment and ascertain the impact on his flock. Yet at the same time that he managed the entire herd, he had an eye for each individual sheep. He skillfully rescued a struggling ewe, saved a newborn's life, and got back to the larger crisis at hand.

Wilderness stories in the Pentateuch characterize God as the Guiding Shepherd. Israel's Divine Pastor led his people through the wilderness by pillars of cloud and fire. He made a pathway through the Red Sea, and eventually led his people safely to their haven of rest.[a] Numbers appears to be a book about aimless wandering, but the summary in chapter thirty-three reveals God leading with purpose. Detours were a result of the community's unwillingness to follow God's direction and timing.[b]

What strikes me most in these accounts is God's willingness to work with his people, even in their mistakes, moving them toward his overall plan. Forty extra years in the desolation of the wilderness were tacked onto the itinerary because of disobedience. But God stayed near, guiding them day and night. He was determined to bring their children into the land of promise. Throughout their sojourn God kept his vision for the community before them.[c]

---

a. Ps. 77:19-20; 78:53-54 b. Num. 13-14 c. Num. 34-35

Along with the pillars, guidance in the wilderness period also took the form of frequent consultation between God and Moses outside the Divine Shepherd's "tent of meeting." I can imagine Israel's leader stepping carefully toward the opening of the sacred tent, waiting respectfully for specific instructions about particular issues faced by the community. Divine wisdom was made accessible on a case-by-case basis.

The crowning, permanent expression of God's guidance was the Torah he delivered through Moses. With a divine signature, this blueprint for community life would provide ongoing direction for succeeding generations. The Torah mapped out a mission for God's people and practical applications of its moral vision. Using a convention common for ancient Near Eastern kings, God's laws were embedded in a covenant relationship intended to ensure their well-being.

Direct divine guidance in the wilderness was obvious and dramatic. But delegation to trusted human shepherds was also essential to God's plan. Though Deuteronomy 32:12 says, "The LORD alone led Israel," Psalm 77:20 reflects on the human instruments: "You led your people like a flock *by the hand of Moses and*

Aaron." This "divine preference for human agency" is a principle we'll want to reflect on more in the days ahead.[2]

I discovered God's interest in using me to guide others one high-school summer at Camp Meadowrun. As a camp counselor I was responsible for a group of fifth grade boys, one of whom had Asperger's syndrome.

Franky Moore had idiosyncrasies. He ate a special lunch. He wouldn't join in group activities. He talked to himself constantly. Antisocial habits coupled with obesity made Franky an easy target for fifth-grade humor. However, Franky's uncanny ability to recount facts kept his fellow campers in awe. If you asked Franky who won the World Series in 1967, he would rattle off not only who played and who won, but also the names of the pitchers and the final score. If you didn't stop him, he would tell you about every game in the series. In any year.

I didn't try to push Franky to do activities he shied away from. I let the current of the group's interests move him along with us. But I really wanted Franky to enjoy swimming with the group. Although he knew how to swim, every afternoon that we went to the pool Franky refused to go in. When I asked him to join us he would say, "My mom says I have to put on my swimsuit, but I don't *have* to swim." He would just circle the pool on his tip toes, belly bouncing with each step, repeating this pat answer to himself.

One day as Franky was circling I got inspired to try a new tactic. I got down on my knees in his pathway and purposely disrupted his routine. "Franky," I asked, "will you go swimming today?"

"My mom says I have to put on my swimsuit, but I don't have to swim."

"I know Franky. You don't have to swim."

"That's right. I don't have to swim. My mom says I don't have to."

"Franky, I know you don't *have* to swim; you *get* to swim."

Franky seemed disconcerted by the variation in our well-practiced dialog. A small crowd of fellow campers was now waiting to see how the conversation would turn out.

"I don't have to swim," he repeated.

"But you *get* to swim," I continued. We tried these new lines out a few more times.

Then Franky Moore's face took on an unusual look of pleasure. He announced with conviction, "I don't *have* to swim. I *get* to swim." He repeated his new mantra and then, before an astonished little crowd, jumped into the pool! You should have heard the applause.

I can still remember Franky's beaming face bobbing up to the water's surface after his first jump. "It's cold, Tim!" he yelled, treading water vigorously.

"I know Franky. But after you get used to it, you'll like it."

"I already like it, Tim."

I tell this story because it was an occasion in my life when I had to figure out how to lead someone who wasn't fully enjoying the benefits of life in our small flock. Rather than letting him wander in circles, God led Franky by my hand into a new way of thinking and experiencing life.

Every day for the remainder of the summer Franky joined our group in the pool. He was no longer on the margins.

I trust that our explorations in the days ahead will promote some good reflection on what it means to guide people in God's ways using God's wisdom.

Come, follow me.

—Matthew 4:19

Following the Leader

On more than one day we've noticed a group of sheep and goats following a shepherd. Shepherds usually lead by walking in front of the flock with an occasional look behind them, using a whistle or special call to keep the horde in line. The notion of "leading" a flock comes from this obvious physical reality of being in front.

I remember one shepherd who assumed that my questions about shepherding would best be answered if I just spent the day alone with his flock. "Just take them out some day and you'll learn what it's all about."

"But," I protested, "I can't take them out. If I walk out of the pen in the morning, none of them will follow me!"

My shepherd friend admitted that I was right. His relational history with the flock ensured what we might call "followership."

While the shepherd's famous out-front position is typical, we will also find occasions when a shepherd is beside or, more often, behind the flock. God told David, for example, "I took you from the pasture and from behind the flock."[a] The shepherd prophet Amos said, "The LORD took me from following the flock."[b]

a. 2 Sam. 7:8 (author's translation) b. Amos 7:15 (NASB)

I asked shepherds what made them change their position, assuming that several hundred animals became virtually leaderless without someone out front. The answers were illuminating.

When the flocks are out in the open wilderness they naturally follow their human source of provision and protection. But when they are traveling through agricultural areas or spaces without good visibility, the shepherds often go to the back to drive them, since a shepherd can be charged a fine for animals grazing in someone's farmland; they have to keep the hungry livestock moving. The back position, along with constant shouts to continue moving, keeps the animals from distraction. The ones in the front feel the pressure of the flock's movement from the rear.

Another occasion for driving the sheep from the back is the long journey to a new pasture or campsite. Sometimes the fatigued flocks have to be "pushed" to a destination against their will.

Three key Hebrew verbs are used for leading a flock. *Nahal* means leading with tenderness and can refer to bringing a flock to a place of rest and refreshment.

Nakhah is a straightforward guidance verb. *Nahag* suggests the kind of directive herding accomplished best from the back of the flock, when the will of the shepherd has to be imposed.[1] These three verbs express the kind of leadership God provided for his people in Scripture and the kind of leadership he expected from anointed shepherds.[2]

I found these verbs prominent in accounts of the Exodus: "The LORD went ahead of them in a cloud pillar to guide (*nakhah*) them on their way."[a] "In your strength you gently led (*nahal*) them to your holy habitation."[b] "But he led forth his own people like sheep and directed (*nahag*) them in the wilderness like a flock."[c]

I also found the same terms used in messages of hope for a Second Exodus written for a community that would face exile: "They will neither hunger nor thirst, nor will the desert heat or the sun beat upon them. He who has compassion on them will guide (*nahag*) them and lead (*nahal*) them beside springs of water."[d] "He will gently lead (*nahal*) those that are with young."[e] "The LORD will guide (*nakhah*) you always; he will satisfy your needs in a sun-scorched land."[f] God was pictured as the kind of shepherd who varied his leadership style to ensure that his treasured flock would make it safely home.

The Twenty-Third Psalm describes God's personalized shepherd leadership with two of these verbs: "He leads (*nahal*) me beside quiet waters" in verse 2, and in verse 3, "He guides (*nakhah*) me in paths of righteousness." We've returned to this Shepherd Psalm throughout our journey, but one essential and obvious assumption in the famous lyrics hasn't gotten much attention yet. The writer, traditionally identified as King David, acknowledged that he was a sheep. Though appointed shepherd of the nation, he was in various ways led, guided, and directed as one of God's flock. We have reflected often on being shepherd leaders, but the Twenty-

a. Exod. 13:21 b. Exod. 15:13 (author's translation) c. Ps. 78:52 (author's translation) d. Isa. 49:10
e. Isa. 40:11 f. Isa. 58:11

Third Psalm is a reminder that we are both shepherds and sheep. Biblically, *leading begins with being led.*

Even the Good Shepherd found it necessary to be led. Jesus frequently sought counsel from his Heavenly Guide and openly stated that he did nothing except as the Father directed him.[a] In his Good Shepherd parable Jesus declared that he would lay down his life for the sheep at his Father's command.[b] Although he was in great anguish prior to his death, the Good Shepherd prayed, "Not my will, but yours be done."[c]

This day has prompted us to reflect both on leading and being led.

First, let's consider our leadership positions and dispositions. Being out front is a striking image of leadership-by-influence. To have won the loyalty of a group of people to such an extent that they follow you wherever you go is an amazing accomplishment. But we can't settle into being up front all the time. Shepherd leaders know when to push from behind because we understand distraction and fatigue. Sometimes we need to guide by the side.

Let's analyze our preference for a particular style in our positions of leadership. Is this style a default set simply by our temperaments or by our job descriptions? Perhaps we need to become more flexible as the environment changes or as the flock's energy level ebbs. Sometimes "bringing up the rear" can give us a needed perspective on why some in the group aren't keeping up.

Now let's reflect on being led. Being in front most of the time can easily inflate our sense of self-importance. But understanding first that we are followers curbs our self-aggrandizing impulses. We need to know what it feels like to follow before we can lead others well.

---

a. John 8:28 b. John 10:18 c. Luke 22:42

Do we follow our Heavenly Shepherd in daily obedience, even when his directives run contrary to our instincts? Do we genuinely see ourselves both as sheep and shepherds? Do we learn about leadership in the process of being led by God's Spirit?

Followership is the beginning—and end—of effective leadership.

He guides me in paths of righteousness.

—Psalm 23:3

Righteous Ruts

𝔞 It happened on an inauspicious July day in 2005:

First one sheep jumped to its death. Then another and another, and then dozens more. Having left their herds to graze while they ate breakfast, stunned Turkish shepherds now watched as nearly *1,500* others leapt off the same cliff. The first 450 animals died under the billowy pile.[1]

How could the shepherds have been so powerless to stop the charge of so many sheep over the cliff? The tragedy happened plainly because the sheep were allowed to wander onto the wrong trail. Unaware of what lay ahead, each one simply followed the next only to perish in the valley below. It is a curious behavior of sheep that once one picks a trail, the rest simply follow the *tail* in front of them without regard for their destination.

Good shepherds lead their flocks on the right paths. This kind of guidance requires knowing the environment well enough to recognize where each trail leads. The valued lives of one's flock depend on guidelines.

As I dug into ancient literature, I found the shepherd's trail to be a common image for a leader's laws. Twentieth century BC King Iddin Dagan believed he was commissioned by his god "to keep the people on the track." In the familiar image of Psalm 23, the Divine Shepherd guides the psalmist on the right trails, on "paths of righteousness." These are the "righteous ruts" or tracks that lead us safely out to pasture and safely home again. Trail imagery in the Bible celebrates normative patterns for godly behavior. Walking in God's *ways* or on his *paths* means following his directions. These divine directives alone secure a flock's safety. The testimony in another Psalm is, "My steps have held to your paths; my feet have not slipped."[a]

God's laws are referred to as *Torah*, a term that can also mean teaching. Torah is the secure path, the right trail on which God's people walk. The commandments of Scripture are the tracks of the Divine Shepherd. God warned ancient Israel not to deviate to the left or the right.[b] The prayer of our ancient

a. Ps. 17:5 b. Deut. 5:32

liturgy is, "Teach me, O LORD, *your path*."[a] A person "in whose heart are highways" has internalized God's path.[b]

God's laws represent the only way of life in a confusing desert of well-worn paths. Ancient Israel forfeited her nationhood because, in God's words, "My people have forgotten Me...They have stumbled from their ways, from the ancient paths, to walk in bypaths."[c] Israel had followed other gods who left them scattered and vulnerable, wandering dangerously in the wilderness of exile. They had lost their way, forsaking the Shepherd who had proven himself a faithful guide. The Lord led them "through the barren wilderness, through a land of deserts and rifts, a land of drought and darkness,[2] a land where no one travels and no one lives."[d] To those in exile who had "gone astray" and "turned to their own ways"[e] came words of hope that God would once again provide a "way in the wilderness."[f]

At Mount Sinai God designed a society with righteous ruts. The Torah's laws would be a witness to his wisdom before the nations:

> Observe them carefully, for this will show your wisdom and understanding to the nations, who will hear about all these decrees and say, "Surely this great nation is a wise and understanding people...*what other nation is so great as to have such righteous decrees and laws as this body of laws I am setting before you today?*" (Deut. 4:6–8)

Rules have the potential to preserve life and to make it flourish: "For I command you today to love the LORD your God, to walk in his ways, and to keep his commands, decrees and laws; *then you will live and increase*, and the LORD your God will bless you in the land you are entering to possess."[g]

---

a. Ps. 27:11 (author's translation) b. Ps. 84:5 (author's translation) c. Jer. 18:15 (NASB) d. Jer. 2:6
e. Isa. 53:6 f. Isa. 40:3 g. Deut. 30:16

I'm left wondering about the righteous tracks or "habits of the heart" on which we as followers travel. What normative behavior blueprint or "rule of life" have we privately set for ourselves, before God, no matter who is looking? Is meditation on Scripture a daily practice? Reflective and intercessory prayer? Do we intentionally seek the wise counsel of others who are steeped in God's word? All of us need some good "ruts"—well-marked paths that we follow even when the tails of our closest companions veer onto tempting bypaths.

Now let's reflect on our leadership in these areas. What just paths or trails of righteousness have we established in our communities? Is it clear what it means to "stay on track"? To flourish, people require wise and carefully thought-out processes, policies, procedures, and protocols. They need thorough orientation and regular reorientation to expected standards of conduct. They benefit from clear and consistently enforced—and regularly reviewed—rules. We all need the benefits of righteous ruts without the drag of needless bureaucracy.

I've seen people thrive with good rules, and I've seen them flounder without guidelines. Honestly, I know some sheep who just can't stay on track, even when it is clearly marked for them.

People walk on the right trails when they have wise guides who understand that education is a constant expression of good leadership. Let's review the written and unwritten guidelines that serve as pathways for our church, our business, or our family. Remember that well-worn trails are easy to follow. But so are others' tails.

Are our sheep safely guided on the righteous ruts, or are they liable to wander off a cliff?

Stand firm in one spirit,
striving as one soul in the faith."

—Philippians 1:27

Working Together

♌ I've noticed that the most demanding work often becomes a forge for life's deepest friendships. Being coworkers through crises and transitions—along with the daily grind—creates a bond as close as family ties. I find this dynamic among those who spend hot days and cold nights caring together for the various and constant needs of a flock. Interestingly, the same Hebrew consonants can spell either "shepherd" or "friend."[1]

Though a shepherd's life involves many solitary hours, a great deal of the work is shared. Since biblical times raising animals in the Middle East has traditionally been family business. To subsist, a family might keep from thirty to fifty sheep and goats and a small farm. With a flock of one hundred or more, pastoralists can generate a surplus of products for trade. However, these rewards only come as a result of hard work by every member in the family—male and female, young and old alike.[a] "Here lies a loose hierarchy based on age...yet in many ways the shepherds are all equal. [They] have to live, work, and breathe together. Cooperation spells survival."[2]

---

a. Gen. 24:13ff; 29:6ff. 37:2; Exod. 2:16; 1 Sam. 16:11; 17:15

I've seen children as young as six years old fully engaged in shepherding tasks. Hired help is integrated into the family team. The result is a remarkable synergy of collaborative effort, especially in the spring when the activities of shearing, birthing, milking, and moving all converge.

In many cases the hired help actually become members of the extended family. They share in all the tasks and are provided for by the products of the flocks. Suhair, whom I met deep in the Negev, said his family name was given by the family his grandparents had worked for. I had heard of "fictive kinship" before. Here was a living example of this ancient tradition of virtual adoption. Their shared solidarity in common work merged their distinct families into a single identity.

Jesus defined his true family as those that kept his will. Pointing to his committed followers, he said, "Here are my mother and brothers."[a] The apostle Paul shared the same camaraderie and family bond with his coworkers in his church planting ministry.[3] At the close of his letter to the Romans, he commends "sister" Phoebe who had been such a help to him and so many others. He greets Prisca and Aquila, a couple who had "risked their necks" for him, and Mary, remembered for her hard work. Paul's kin Andronicus and Junias had become "fellow prisoners." Other "fellow workers in the LORD" include Urbanus, Tryphaena, and Tryphosa.

a. Matt. 12:46–50

Stachys, like another hard worker Persis, is "beloved." The list mentions thirty people by name with different designations, all of which reflect the intimacy and joy that result from laboring side-by-side in this world's most significant work.[a]

The church is a single unit that "grows and builds itself up in love, *as each part does its work*."[b] Early in Paul's epistle to the Philippians he encouraged the believers to exhibit unity in their work, to "stand firm in one spirit, striving as one soul in the faith."[c] He was grieved when two of his Philippian colleagues were at odds with each other: "I urge Euodia and I urge Syntyche to live in harmony in the LORD. Indeed, *true comrade*, I ask you also to help these women who have *shared my struggle* in the cause of the gospel, together with Clement also and the rest of *my fellow workers*, whose names are in the book of life."[d] Getting along was essential for the progress of the work.

The biblical call to collegial co-laboring among such a diverse group of people is grounded in a belief that leaders are called to serve *God's* flock together. They have the same Owner to whom they each give account. Peter exhorts fellow elders to, "Be shepherds of God's flock...and when the Chief Shepherd appears, you will receive the crown of glory that will never fade away."[e]

---

a. Rom. 16 b. Eph. 4:16 c. Phil. 1:27 (author's translation) d. Phil. 4:2–3 (NASB) e. 1 Pet. 5:2–4

My wife and I experienced the exhilaration and camaraderie that comes from starting a school together with like-minded folks. Many have had this experience with a church plant. The vision drives you to countless hours and unthinkable sacrifice. I remember a reporter asking me how much time Maureen and I had spent on average each week during the year before the school opened.

Without much thought I said, "Maybe from ten to fifteen hours each." She responded, "You've got to be kidding! It must be a lot more than that." "Maybe," I replied. "It's just that no one's counting."

Paul said, "I thank my God every time I think of you."[a] Let's take some time to recall with gratitude the deep friendships that have been formed in the context of ministry. Some were likely forged when the work was the hardest and the crises were the most urgent. Now we think of these individuals as "friends that stick closer than a brother."[b]

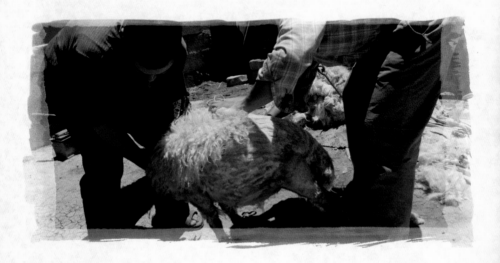

a. Phil. 1:3 (cf. Col. 1:3; 1 Thess. 1:2) b. Prov. 18:24

In the shepherd's family business there is an appreciation for what each member is best suited to do. There are allowances for weaknesses and expectations for strengths. To what extent does this flexible family dynamic characterize our spiritual communities? What are the impediments to it?

How is the "team spirit" these days? Do members *feel* like family? What are the external challenges or interpersonal threats to good working harmony? Sometimes our ministry experience feels too much like a *dysfunctional* family.

The effectiveness of leaders is often determined by how they mobilize a team of coworkers to share the same vision and passion for the work at hand. Three questions might help us assess whether or not we are likely to have a truly shared vision. First, is the burden we expect others to share consuming us first? Second, is the work shared enough so that others are not simply watching us do most of the labor? Finally, is it clear that joining us in self-sacrificial service is an expression of loyalty not so much to us personally, but to the Chief Shepherd?

The princes of the earth—rams, lambs, goats and bulls.

—Ezekiel 39:18

Indigenous Leadership

It always amazes me when I come upon a shepherd with hundreds of animals alone in the wilderness. Imagine exercising any control over such a mob, especially with so many needs and potential mishaps. And once the flock arrives at a grazing stop, the animals scatter into small clusters and begin to wander. Especially the goats.

Over time I discovered the key: Shepherds co-opt indigenous leadership. They empower natural leaders within a flock. Often ninety percent of a herd consists of ewes (female sheep). These are by nature docile followers, keeping their heads down and following the tails in front of them. The rams (male sheep) are more aggressive and aware of their environment. A wise shepherd needs to understand these inborn traits.

I remember once trying to photograph a group of ewes. A handful of rams instinctively formed a protective blockade between me and the flock. While they fight amongst themselves for the "butting order," they usually form a tier of leadership that shepherds can count on.

The goats are another story. They don't "flock." True to their independent nature, they take off in search of random foliage. Two brothers from the Beni Sakhr tribe illustrate this. Hisham herds sheep and Amjad herds goats. Amjad laughed, "They never let me rest. They just keep moving and getting into trouble. My brother's job is easy." During the afternoon, my interview with Hisham went uninterrupted. Amjad hardly sat down.

Though goats cause the most hassle for shepherds, one can see their value during a march between pastures. The goats provide leadership. Sometimes they trot along the edges of the flock like sergeants keeping the troops in order.

On another occasion, I was quite impressed with a goat that apparently took charge of order at feeding time. He stood in the middle of several feeding troughs while the sheep rushed to feed—pretty impressive for an animal famous for its reckless independence.

Other kinds of leaders form in a flock. The shepherd may train a special lamb to represent him. In Jordan they call this a *mariá*. Often a female, it is bonded at birth with the donkey, another member of the "leadership team." If the shepherd takes a portion of the flock to a watering hole or leaves in search of some laggers, the donkey or the *mariá* may be left with the others. The flock is satisfied with the substitute.

I once saw a good sized herd near the Jordan Valley milling in the hot sun without a shepherd. A water source flowed nearby, but they were surprisingly orderly, apparently waiting for some kind of signal. Among them stood the shepherd's donkey. When the shepherd returned, I asked how long he could expect the flock to respect his stand-in, especially knowing that their peers were slaking their thirst a few hundred yards away. To my astonishment he said two days! I expected he might say twenty minutes, but two days?

The most memorable lesson I learned came while watching rabbinical students at Neot Keddumim, a center for researching nature and the Bible. The students were asked to guide a flock of thirteen sheep and goats across a pen with three stipulations: the animals couldn't touch the fence, they had to cross a little bridge in the center of the enclosure, and the participants couldn't physically move the flock. Three or four students at a time entered the pen, only to find the flock scatter irretrievably. None of them could mobilize this small group of animals (though some tried bribing with snack food). The key was an unimposing ewe who apparently possessed the natural leadership in this flock. She was just waiting for someone to make eye contact with her and begin walking. She would've followed with the rest behind—even the goats!

It might come as a surprise that goats—infamous for being the self-centered people on the left (bad) side of the Shepherd Judge in Matthew 25—are also symbols for leaders in the Bible. After a generation of exile, God exhorted a community to flee Babylon, to "be like the goats at the head of the flock."[a] Most

---

a. Jer. 50:8

readers don't know that behind the English word *leader* in some Old Testament passages is the Hebrew word for male goat or buck (*'attud*). God says in Zechariah, "My anger burns against the shepherds, and I will punish the *leaders* (bucks); for the LORD Almighty will care for his flock."[a] The terms for shepherds and bucks are parallel, suggesting similar work.

The Bible shows God's preference for diverse and indigenous leaders. Beside epic leaders such as Moses, Deborah, David, Jesus, and Paul, we find supporting leaders such as Aaron and Miriam, Barak, Jonathan, Mary Magdalene, and Barnabas. Mordecai and Esther took turns leading each other, switching roles in a national crisis.

Countless nameless elders also make up the local decision-making corps. Ephesians 4:11 describes the special gifting of apostles, prophets, evangelists, and teaching pastors, but articulates their role as the equipping of *God's people* for the work of service.[b] Local churches, overseen by elders and deacons, were to be hubs of ministry activity. The image of the body in 1 Corinthians 12 suggests that each individual provides uniquely gifted leadership to the other members of the body.

As we reflect on various organizational settings, can we equate with one type of leadership or another? In two contexts I discovered that I'm a goat. Thankfully, this didn't dawn on me until after I realized that goat-like tendencies could be good. Though independence sometimes gets me into trouble, it also prompts others to follow.

In situations where I am the shepherd, I have sometimes been impatient with goats. Independent thinkers can slow group process down. I wonder if we're willing to give some freedom to the goats, though they sometimes require more

---

a. Zech. 10:3 (cf. Isa. 14:9) b. Eph. 4:12

energy to lead. The Bedouin are right: "You can't live with them, and you can't live without them."

As leaders, how are we taking advantage of the natural, indigenous leadership in our flocks? Do we watch closely to identify the rams? Have we recognized leadership gifts among the ewes—those who may not have dominant personalities?

Are some, like the donkey and *mariá*, so closely associated with us that they easily get the others to follow? Perhaps we can promote this association more explicitly.

In the end, leadership is never reducible to an individual. Leadership is a shared dynamic in any community or organization. *Shared* leadership is a reality in a flock and a biblical norm for the church.

*They will keep you from being ineffective
and unproductive in your knowledge
of our LORD Jesus Christ.*

—2 Peter 1:8

Productivity

𝕝 Perhaps because of the parable of the lost sheep and the ninety-nine, we tend to imagine relatively small herds. I was awed the first time I witnessed four hundred sheep with a shepherd. Then I saw two thousand. Even this number pales in comparison to flocks in other parts of the Middle East.

Domestication of sheep and goats occurred long before civilization, and their products have been major components of economies in the region until this day. Royal herds in antiquity numbered in the hundreds of thousands. Twenty-first century BC accounts of flocks in the ancient city of Ur number 350,000 animals! Annual consumption by the courts of ancient Ebla once required 70–80,000 herd animals. Spectacular banquets on record include 25,000 sheep. Slaughter for religious rituals required the raising of still more. A primary motive for war was to raid the livestock of neighbors to support these enormous demands. Egyptian King Thutmose carried off over 20,000 sheep in the battle of Megiddo in the fifteenth century BC. Ramses II later boasted of seizing tens of thousands of herd animals from the Hittites.[1]

I came to discover that these vast herds were not just raised for killing. As the "gift that keeps on giving," these flocks provided a fresh and almost endless supply of fiber and milk products.

I heard the Bedouin sometimes call their flocks *hallal*. This term caught me by surprise because I recognized it as an adjective. *Hallal* means good and pure—a description of the products of the sheep as well as their temperaments. Sheep have provided the world with wool for centuries. Up to three pounds of this strong, warm, and fire retardant commodity can be sheared each year for clothing, rugs, pillows, and mattresses.[2] Wool absorbs moisture (including dyes) well and "breathes." Goats are also shorn yearly. Their hair becomes ropes and blankets and the black sewn panels of the traditional desert tent most visible at any campsite. God's tent, the Tabernacle, was woven primarily from goat hair.

Both animals are reliable sources of fresh milk in hot regions without refrigeration. A healthy ewe might supply over 25 gallons of high-fat milk annually. The white gold is converted into curd, butter, fat (for candles, soap, etc.), and a wide variety of yogurts and cheeses (up to 35 percent fat and 25 percent protein). When treated properly, cheese can last indefinitely. One form called *kishk*, dried and salted, can still be eaten after ten years—if you add a little water! Goats produce up to 50 percent more milk than sheep, though with less fat it is valued less. Another byproduct results when animals graze in the fields after harvest and their droppings replace important nutrients in the soil.

Eventually flock animals make their final contribution—they are slaughtered for food. Mutton is a rare treat among Middle Eastern shepherds, usually reserved for special occasions. I'll never forget eating a slaughtered lamb with a Bedouin host who presented it with the fat tail and skull on top of the meat. The tail is a 100 percent fat delicacy that we were obligated to eat—and pretend to enjoy! Priests in biblical times were allotted these cherished tails as a valued source of fat in Israel's otherwise lean diet."[a]

Once slaughtered, the meat is only one of an animal's final products. As one observer quipped, "Everything is used except the bleat."[3] The blood had a central symbolic function in religious ritual. Horns became instruments for making sounds for war or worship or for carrying small objects. Bones became tools. Dried and sewn skins from both animals were used for carrying liquid (as ancient water jugs) and as churns. Armies used inflated sheepskins to ford rivers. Skins were also used for clothing or, if tanned, the leather could be turned into parchment.

Those of us in industrialized cultures may find it hard to appreciate the unique value of herd animals in traditional Middle Eastern societies. Flocks are prized capital with regular "dividends" of milk and fiber. They have been called "bank accounts on foot," "mobile meat lockers," and "self-propelled cheese factories." And they manage this, for the most part, by grazing on vegetation that grows naturally beyond the farmlands. An anthropologist friend once said of goats, "They produce meat out of dry thorns!"[4]

---

a. Lev. 7:1–6

I find spiritual productivity to be both pervasive and completely organic in Scripture, not something generated out of human activity. Peter provides a list of divinely empowered qualities and then concludes, "For if you possess these qualities in increasing measure, they will keep you from being ineffective and *unproductive* in your knowledge of our LORD Jesus Christ."[a] Elsewhere the Holy Spirit is identified as the source of spiritual productivity. The fruits of the Holy Spirit are "love, joy, peace, patience, kindness, goodness, faithfulness, gentleness, and self-control."[b] The Spirit's desire is to make us *fruit-full.*

The Holy Spirit is the source of another kind of product—spiritual gifts:

> But to each one is given the manifestation of the Spirit for the common good. For to one is given the word of wisdom through the Spirit, and to another the word of knowledge according to the same Spirit; to another faith by the same Spirit, and to another gifts of healing by the one Spirit, and to another the effecting of miracles, and another prophecy, and to another the distinguishing of spirits, to another various kinds of tongues, and to another the interpretation of tongues. But one and the same Spirit works all these things, distributing to each one individually just as He wills. (1 Cor. 12:7–11)

The gifts, like the fruit of the Spirit, serve the good of the community. God's flock is to be *hallal*—good both in temperament and in productivity. With the proper spiritual nutrition, Christians become sources of life-giving products to others.

I'm afraid we have misused the term *productivity* to mean busyness or activity. Rather, our interest should be in the life of the Spirit expressing itself in Christlike character. Can we recognize the fruits and gifts of the Holy Spirit in our

a. 2 Pet. 1:8 b. Gal. 5:22 (cf. Phil. 1:11; Col. 1:10)

own lives? Perhaps now is the time to ask trusted colleagues for feedback on our *spiritual* productivity.

Images of spiritual productivity are reminders that God has a purpose for blessing us. Yes, he cares about our health and well-being, *but ultimately his purpose is to bless others through us.* Can we identify ways in which the Lord has resourced us so that we might resource others? Are people nourished by our spiritual products?

Let me rotate the lens to focus on our leadership. Are we driving our flocks to religious activity or encouraging healthy spiritual productivity? Is a wide variety of products appreciated and developed? Put differently—are we really interested in what the Holy Spirit has given to the church? Serious reflection on these questions may keep us from being "ineffective and unproductive in our knowledge of our LORD Jesus Christ."

Be fruitful and multiply, and fill the earth.

—Genesis 1:28

Reproduction

♌ Whenever we were out in the fields taking pictures of sheep, I found the shepherds always intent on showing off their best rams. I might be interested in spotted and speckled sheep, nursing ewes, or frolicking kids. But they would motion for me to wait, quickly grab the horns of their favorite ram, and pose for a picture. I understood why they were so proud of the males. In a herd that was usually about 90 percent female, the rams and bucks were kept for breeding. The majority of the young male lambs and kids were usually sold off. The few they kept were promising studs. With a ratio of about one male to ten females, the future of the flock's growth was equated with the virility of these males.

A shepherd's interest in production is ultimately expressed in efforts to ensure successful reproduction. An ancient poem describes shepherds "toiling long to make them countless."[1] Ideally and quite intentionally, an owner attempts to double the herd size annually. He wants "all of them to bear twins, and none to lose her young."[a] With enough food and water, a flock can have two breeding seasons each year. During heat shepherds pay careful attention to which animals are mating and which aren't. They try to ensure that every ewe is pregnant. However,

---

a. Song 4:2 (author's translation.)

the 100 percent ideal is hardly ever realized, and never as an average over several years. Though some females will give twins, others will miscarry. With the deaths of mothers and newborns, diseases and predators, the selling off of weaned males to pay expenses and help, and the unpredictable supply of water and vegetation, a flock may only average a 10 percent growth in size annually. The odds for this or better depend on the shepherd's skilled ability to work with nature.

A productive and reproductive flock parallels the blessed life God encouraged among humans in Genesis 1:28: "Be *fruitful* and *multiply*, and fill the earth." He repeats this "Creation Mandate" to Noah after the flood destroyed the world.[a]

The multiplication of sheep and goats is a sign of blessing in the Bible, while decimation of a herd is a curse.[2] God promised his tent-dwelling community a "land flowing with milk and honey," a select environment for raising flocks and planting farms. This was the land through which God brought Abraham when he first made the promise. Abraham grew such enormous herds that he and Lot had to move into separate regions. As a pastoralist wealthy in mobile assets, Abraham had access to the courts of kings. His grandson Jacob was also a successful shepherd. In spite of Laban's attempts to prolong his status as a dependent in the household, Jacob managed to grow his own flocks and eventually move away.

The story of Jacob and the dark, spotted, and speckled animals in Genesis 30 has fascinated commentators for generations. Is it a story of superstition, divine intervention, or the shrewdness of an experienced herder? For pay Jacob asks his uncle to give him only the sheep that are not all white and the goats that are not all black. His request is for less than the 10 to 20 percent a herder was entitled to

---

a. Gen. 9:1

in contracts of the period. Laban agrees, but then takes the dark, spotted, and the speckled and puts them under the care of his own sons.[a] This is one of the many ways Jacob is cheated by his uncle.

But Jacob is still in charge of Laban's flocks. He "encourages" the breeding of the stronger females when they are in heat by putting fresh cut and peeled branches from poplar, almond, and plane trees in the watering troughs. The purported effect of the toxic substances in these particular trees was to hasten the estrus cycle. They were viewed as aphrodisiacs.[3] As Jacob hoped, the males responded to the ewes that were placed near the troughs, and the result was miraculous. The strong animals gave birth to dark, spotted, and speckled offspring. However, the real secret of Jacob's success was not in his unusual strategy and techniques. These were only the means, revealed in a dream,[b] for *God* to provide the blessing of multiplication. Reproduction is ultimately the result of divine intervention.

a. Gen. 30:34–36   b. Gen. 31:10–13

A spiritual meaning is given to a flock's multiplication in Jeremiah, a prophet who seemed to have an unusual familiarity with pastoral realities.[4] He promises to a nation on the verge of exile and possible extinction, "I will bring them back to their pasture and they will be fruitful and multiply." [a] These words echo the creation directive for a community facing death and deprivation. God would replace barrenness with creative energy and new life.

The New Testament echoes the Creation Mandate in the "Great Commission": "Therefore go and make disciples of all nations."[b] The disciples were to multiply followers of Jesus throughout the earth. The story of how that began is in the book of Acts. On over a dozen pivotal occasions we read that the *numbers* of believers *increased*. The size of the flock grew wherever the gospel was preached. Gentile newcomers were the "other sheep" Jesus had referred to in John 10:16.

a. Jer. 23:3 (author's translation.) b. Matt. 28:19

When we are healthy and well-resourced, reproduction is natural. One question we need to answer is whether or not we are personally reproducing ourselves. Are we bringing into this world new life in others?

In our ministries, are we coaching evangelism and modeling discipleship? Are we helping our colleagues understand reproduction as natural and organic? Have we fully communicated the idea that *leading is breeding*?

Let's put the concern for growth in perspective. If our congregation is not growing numerically, is it for lack of intentional focus and organized effort or for lack of spiritual health? While a flock's reproduction is natural, shepherds need attentive awareness to opportune moments, to "breeding season." The goal for every shepherd is 100 percent reproduction—the same goal as the Owner's.

Be shepherds of God's flock that is under your care.

—1 Peter 5:2

Think Flock

 Ⴟ "*Think flock*, Tim."

Once Rivka said it, I could tell a new insight about shepherding was about
to come into focus.

Rivka had immigrated to Israel in the 1960s—young and idealistic,
energetic about living close to the land. She and her family were goat herders for
several years in the biblical Wilderness of Judea. They learned much from the native
Bedouin shepherds camped nearby. It was a hard life that brought little income but
some important lessons. She taught me one during an interview at her clinic. Now a
full-time veterinarian, Rivka told me that my questions reflected an almost exclusive
interest in individual animals—their habits, needs, and diseases. To understand
shepherding I needed a different frame of reference. I needed to "think flock."

While herders care intimately for each of their animals, they are equally
preoccupied with the status of the whole herd. To "think flock" means to make
decisions with a priority on the welfare of the collective whole. Shepherds manage
water and food resources in an unpredictable ecological environment. They negotiate
trading and sales arrangements. They reassess travel routes in light of weather and
safety. They manage their help.

The bigger the flock size, the higher the stakes in these decisions. At a certain threshold size and during specific seasons, some shepherds spend more time managing the affairs of a flock than personally caring for them. One Bedouin says, "A successful live-stock-raiser today has to be a good manager. He has to arrange access to grazing land, provide water, organize

shepherding, procure fodder, obtain veterinarian care and medicine, and make decisions about when and how many animals to sell."[1] The owners have to depend on trusted field shepherds for day-to-day animal husbandry.

I've already noted how enormous flocks could be in antiquity—sometimes numbering hundreds of thousands. I discovered that flock management in the ancient societies of Ur, Uruk, and Ugarit involved three different levels of herders. Along with administrative heads, there were chief contractors, and then field shepherds.[2]

When I inquired among the Bedouin about the herder hierarchy, they always answered simply, "We are *shepherds*." Some were owners, some were family members of the owners, and some were hired help. Despite the necessary division of labor, their preferred term for everyone involved was shepherd. This preference apparently reflected the reality that they all had spent considerable time in the fields with the flocks and would continue to do so as necessary.

As a flock owner of two thousand sheep, Abu-Munir had said to me, "I hired shepherds who handle five hundred head each. But I spend time every day with the animals. Maybe the sick. Maybe the newborns. If I weren't out with the sheep every day, I wouldn't know what they need. I couldn't make good decisions." Though he could have spent more time in a cool, shaded tent, he knew that personal contact with individual animals and sub-groupings would give perspective for managerial oversight of his large herd.

Psalm 23 is a treasured meditation on the Lord as "*my* Shepherd." Appreciating God in such personal terms is biblical, but I've encountered more frequent pastoral references to the corporate whole, to "the *people*[3] of his pasture, the *flock* under his care."[a]

The royal leader in Israel was sometimes called a *nagid*, the very term used in other ancient societies for a chief herd contractor. God promised to his scattered flock in exile that one day, "I will place over them one shepherd, my servant David, and he will tend them; he will tend them and be their shepherd. I the LORD will be their God, and my servant David will be prince (*nagid*) among them."[b] David would be both field shepherd and shepherd king. God wanted him to express his herder's heart in the management of a nation.

Ezekiel's promise was fulfilled by the great Son of David, Jesus Christ. His ministry was marked by an intense focus on twelve disciples, three of whom shared the most intimate bonding. Yet seventy-two disciples were mobilized on at least one occasion.[c] Frequently Jesus taught and ministered to thousands at a time. When he saw these crowds as "sheep without a shepherd," he rallied his disciples as deputy shepherds to manage their feeding.[d]

---

a. Ps. 95:7 (cf. Ps. 74:1; 77:20; 80:1ff.)   b. Ezek. 34:23–24   c. Luke 10:1ff.   d. Mark 6:34ff.

Later on these same disciples would find the work of spiritual shepherding in Jerusalem overwhelming. So they chose capable helpers to manage individual needs while they maintained their focus on the spiritual well-being of the whole flock.[a] Paul's church planting strategy involved managing the growth of numerous new flocks through trained and trusted shepherds in each city. It appears that for the early church leaders, as with Bedouin herders, there was fluid movement between intimate, individual care and strategic, "big picture" flock management.

This topic may be difficult for many of us who went into vocational ministry with a heart for people. We desire to care for them as individuals. However, group dynamics eventually catch up with us. The "church" or "institution" is something bigger than the aggregate collection of its members. It has a macro-identity to be discerned and managed. Sooner or later, we are confronted with hard decisions that concern the interest of the whole, but come at the expense of a person or family. We might find ourselves discussing layoffs in a closed board meeting without giving the affected employees advance notice. We might use public discipline to warn others who are headed down the same trail. I've had to resist the compassionate instinct to bend a good policy for an individual's unique circumstances when the result would be debilitating for everyone. Frankly, "thinking flock" runs against my grain.

Like social workers, many of us enjoy the case work, but not the paperwork. The dreams of spending undisturbed hours preparing sermons collide with the realities of tedious committee meetings, time-consuming capital campaigns, building maintenance, and a host of unexpected crises. We need to manage human and material resources. We have to manage our own time and energy effectively.

a. Acts 6:1–6

Only after several ministry settings and some lengthy Bible study have I grown to understand that management is a significant expression of shepherding. The "I just want to be a shepherd" sentiment often lacks a biblical theology of management. Even a small family requires parental shepherds willing to manage.

As any flock grows, more levels of administration tend to evolve. While the trend toward "flat" organizational diagrams continues, growth typically demands administrative layering. Some pastors of large churches say they have transitioned from shepherds to ranchers. For some, this statement is a remorseful admission that the realities of a large congregation now keep them from being "with the sheep" as much as they once were. One pastor said, "Don't call me your pastor anymore. I was only your shepherd when I could visit each family and perform all of your weddings and funerals."

When I hear these sentiments, I recall the Bedouin preference for the word *shepherd*, no matter how their duties change. *Shepherds* have meetings, discuss budgets, and adapt strategic planning to emerging circumstances. But they insist on contact with their flocks. Like Abu-Munir, they say, "If I weren't out with the sheep every day, I wouldn't know what they need." At least selectively and symbolically, head shepherds should find regular time to be in the field with the sheep. We should embrace the realities of a growing flock without remorse and pay careful attention to our changing roles. But we don't need to abandon our fundamental identity.

We are *shepherds*.

Shepherd the flock of God among you,
not under compulsion, but voluntarily.

—1 Peter 5:2 (NASB)

Finding Good Help

My Jordanian translator, Kamil, and I started out early one morning for interviews. Near a ridge that divided ancient Ammon and Moab, we spotted a large flock grazing. Our approach was greeted by barking dogs, but no shepherd or tent came into sight. Then from the middle of the flock, a weathered man wrapped tightly in a cloak rose from the ground where he had spent the night. He spoke the traditional greeting, *Marhaba* ("You're welcome"), and invited us to join him. After accepting Kamil's explanation for our visit, Abu-Yasmin settled back on the soft earth and invited us to ask questions.

I tried some open-ended queries about shepherding, but he gave brief and predictable responses. (We probably hadn't picked the best time for storytelling!) So I proposed a scenario: "What if I wanted to buy some of your sheep and I asked you to teach me everything I needed to know to care for them? How long would it take? What would the "curriculum" look like?" Apparently, the hypothetical nature of my question was lost on Abu-Yasmin.

However, his ears perked up at the mention of a sale, and he and Kamil launched into an animated discussion without me.

I tried to clarify that I really just wanted to learn about shepherding. Abu-Yasmin looked long and hard at me and gave another cryptic response. Then he and Kamil leaned back in laughter.

"What did he say?!" I protested.

Kamil hesitated to tell me.

After insisting, I finally got the truth: "He says, 'You're *useless!*'"

In Abu-Yasmin's world, you grow up as a shepherd. Bedouin don't write textbooks. They pass on shepherding skills as the need arises and in their rich storytelling lore by the evening fireside. It's caught more than taught.

While the family is the primary workforce, local non-family members might be employed. So my line of questioning now changed to, "What do you look for when you hire from another family? How do you find good help?"

The first answer to this question was transparent already: skill or expertise. Abu-Yasmin's sentiments are echoed by members of the Qashqa'i tribe from Iran

who say, "The quality of the shepherd's herding is immediately apparent to the employer...Unlike some other forms of production, animal husbandry is directly affected by the amount and quality of labor invested."[1]

Without skill a shepherd is useless.

But knowledge of animal husbandry alone is useless. In the words of another herder, "Success as a shepherd requires both skill in recognizing and catering for the animals' needs, and *much hard work*, which should bear fruit in the improved condition of the employer's flock."[2] A poor work ethic is the most common complaint among herd owners.

Yet expertise and hard work are only valuable in combination with a third attribute: trustworthiness. As we've heard before, "It is a common belief among herd owners that shepherds will steal or eat their sheep if given a chance. They demand to see the skin of each sheep that dies or is slaughtered to assure themselves that their livestock is not being sold."[3] When a family's *livelihood* is placed precariously in the hands of workers who, in some regions, leave for months at a time, a skilled, hard-working, trustworthy shepherd is every owner's dream.[4]

I've surveyed the titles and epithets of kings in the ancient world and found the most consistent and widely attested is "faithful shepherd." This designation signaled expertise, hard work, and responsibility before their gods. The Bible celebrates King David as God's chosen servant who "shepherded" God's people "with integrity of heart," who led them "with skillful hands."[a] The Divine Shepherd was looking for trustworthy field hands who would "lead...with knowledge and understanding."[b] Shepherds who understood their role as stewards and servants.

---

a. Ps. 78:72 b. Jer. 3:15

On too many occasions God had trouble finding good help. He condemned the shepherd rulers of Judah for assuming that their role was the basis for entitlement rather than responsibility: "You eat the curds, clothe yourselves with the wool and slaughter the choice animals, but you do not take care of the flock."[a] Though the Bible reveals a "divine preference for human agency,"[5] God promised to personally interrupt this leadership scandal.

The interruption came in the person of the Messiah. By living life with his disciples continuously for three years, Jesus taught them shepherding the Bedouin way. He engaged them in his work among the "lost sheep of Israel."[b] And when they returned from their work, he offered rest and instruction—but not until after they worked some more.[c] In the process he modeled a work ethic and cultivated a sense of personal accountability. In his absence he would trust them to "feed my sheep."[d]

Peter certainly got the message. In a letter written years later to fellow shepherds, he reminds them how to work for the Divine Herd Owner:

> To the elders among you, I appeal as a fellow elder...Be shepherds of *God's* flock that is under your *care*, serving as *overseers*—not because you must, but because you are *willing*, as God wants you to be; *not greedy* for money, but *eager* to serve; not lording it over *those entrusted to you*, but being examples to the flock. (1 Pet. 5:1–3)[6]

A friend of mine began working for a growing ministry and received a rather fluid job description. His written list of duties ended with this item: "Whatever else we ask you to do." He often joked that the list really needed only this item. His boss had insisted on this final line because of the tendency among

---

a. Ezek. 34:3   b. Matt. 10:6   c. Mark 6:30–44   d. John 21:15–17

workers to adopt a "union mentality." He had no interest in hearing the familiar line, "That's not my job." This shepherd wanted someone skilled *and* willing to take responsibility for the work—whatever that was.

Perhaps we've felt that our job description has changed too many times without our say. It is especially common for church leaders to be confronted by an endless list of colliding expectations. Church members consider themselves personal employers of their shepherds.

While it is impossible and unscriptural to accept these expectations, we must resist the union mentality. When I heard flock owners say, "We need someone willing to work hard, to do whatever we need," I sensed God speaking. Shepherd leadership is doing what needs to be done. Shepherd leadership is pushing what's stuck. Shepherd leadership is pitching in when someone's position can't be filled. You cover for weaknesses. You roll with circumstances.

I can't think of any job more constantly redefined than a pastor's (except a parent's). We take responsibility for the development of a group of people, for better or worse, in sunshine and rain.

In God's economy we are stewards and servants. The question is, are we skilled, hard-working, and trustworthy?

As apostles of Christ we might have asserted our authority, but we proved to be gentle among you.

—1 Thessalonians 2:6–7

Authority and Abuse

A tour guide in Israel was once describing the distinctive form of leadership exhibited by shepherds in the Middle East: "With just a simple call or whistle, their obedient flocks fall in behind them." However, most of the people on the bus were watching a very different scene on the nearby hillside with muffled amusement. A man was chasing a small herd of sheep and goats from behind, yelling at them and throwing rocks. The guide was so perturbed that he stopped the bus and told the man how unbefitting his behavior was as a shepherd—and how he had just turned his lecture into a joke. The bewildered man explained that he wasn't a shepherd.

He was a *butcher!*[1]

Telling this story perpetuates the notion that all shepherds are kind and lead simply by gentle words. Unfortunately, I've seen many *shepherds* in the same regions yelling and throwing rocks, smacking them with sticks, and driving their terrorized flocks from behind. That's because not all shepherds are good shepherds.

Shepherds can be impatient with their flocks' behavior, the weather, and grazing options. They can feel overworked and taken advantage of. Perhaps they've been given some sick animals that infect the herd. Perhaps they themselves are sick. Many feel trapped by economic or political circumstances beyond their control.

Some don't have the temperament to lead the best way. For whatever reason, they've chosen the shortcut to a quick response. They yell and throw rocks and beat their animals with a rod.

It's easy to become an abusive shepherd. Once you leave the populated areas, no one is watching. Sheep are utterly defenseless and pitifully dependent. They are not known for their intelligence. Their eyesight is limited to about thirty feet. Most of the time they follow those around them without knowing the destination. They get lost. And stuck. Sometimes you find them "cast"—on their backs and unable to get up. As with so many predicaments, being upended can lead to death within hours. Such neediness can lead a care-giver to cynicism. Sometimes a shepherd lashes out in anger. He might kick one back into line. He might be a little rough with one struggling on its back. He might strike an aggressive one on the head with a stick. It happens out on the field where you can forget you're working for someone else.

If you abuse a flock for long, however, a day of reckoning will come. When sheep are neglected, they won't eat or nurse well. If they're frightened, they will scatter, sometimes beyond reach. Herd owners don't need much time to recognize the negative effects of an abusive field hand on their flocks.

As much as my generation might seek to minimize hierarchical distinctions, the Bible, from beginning to end, promotes a proper use of authority. For example, David was told, "This is what the LORD Almighty says: 'I took you from the pasture and from following the flock to be *ruler over* my people Israel.'"[a] Leaders in both Old and New Testament were "put in charge" or given authority to rule.[b] Paul *commanded* those he led, and he expected church leaders to command those in their charge.[c] He instructed parents and masters to exercise authority over children and servants.[d]

But power easily corrupts. We've already seen this dynamic in David's affair with Bathsheba.

Unfortunately, that affair wasn't the end of the abuse of power in David's line. Ezekiel 34 paints a poignant picture of abusive leaders among David's royal successors a few centuries later. Through the prophet, God blames the condition of the "flock" of Israel on their "shepherds"—that is, their rulers. After detailing the evidence that "you do not take care of the flock,"[e] the focus turns to the abuse of power: "You have ruled them harshly and brutally."[f] The New American Standard version translates the phrase, "With force and with severity you have dominated them."

A little digging reveals an ugly association in this verse. The Hebrew word translated *brutally* or *with severity* is only found in the Old Testament with reference to the conditions of slavery they had experienced in Egypt.[2] The Lord was saying, "Shame on the shepherds for behaving like Israel's former slave owners!"

Jesus found God's people in a similar predicament in his day. His compassion radiated to a crowd that was "*harassed and helpless*, like sheep without

a. 2 Sam. 7:8 b. Acts 6:3 (NASB); I Tim. 5:17 c. 2 Thess. 3:4, 12; I Tim. 1:3; 4:11; 6:17ff; Heb 13:17 d. Eph. 6:1ff. e. Ezek. 34:3 f. Ezek. 34:4b

a shepherd."[a] Jesus was also angry for the same reasons expressed in Ezekiel—abuse of power and lack of concern. The word *helpless* is taken from a Greek verb normally translated "to throw," and here sometimes translated "downcast." Perhaps Jesus had in mind the particularly helpless condition of sheep that are "cast." As a good shepherd, Jesus saw people with compassion. He understood that his power and authority was to be used for their benefit. Paul's perspective was similar in 2 Corinthians 10:8: God gives authority to leaders not for destruction but for edification. The word he uses for destruction literally means "to overthrow." The biblical inclination of power brokers is not to upend people, but rather to empower them.

Unfortunately "shepherding" has been used in some religious circles to justify highly-controlled accountability groups with authoritarian rule. I remember prayerfully helping disengage a person fully enmeshed in an abusive cult group. They dangled his eternal destiny before him whenever he wouldn't share all of his personal thoughts and possessions.

Biblical leadership uses formal authority (based in role) and informal influence (based in relationship) to serve responsibly. We make decisions, set the direction, and, sometimes, determine the destiny of those we lead. The critical question is how we use this incredible power. Do we bully, "pull rank," and terrorize? Do we bring an overbearing or demeaning style to work, perhaps using our position to inflate our own egos? Or do we serve, support, encourage, and empower?

Let's look carefully at the specific forms of abuse likely in our own settings: Discrimination based on gender, race, disability, or disparate views. Sexual harassment. Sarcasm. Lack of checks and balances—and being insulted when they are

---

a. Matt. 9:36

requested. Required forms of deference or "loyalty" that are humiliating or incredibly inconveniencing. Taking special privileges with money. Using public forums to advance personal agendas or vendettas. In Peter's words, we are good shepherds when we are serving willingly and eagerly and "*not lording it over* those entrusted to you."[a] Leadership is not lordship!

Let's push deeper into our own family lives. Perhaps we have learned how to empower and enfranchise others in a ministry setting, but resort to authoritarian impulses with our children. I have. This kind of behavior can be kept from public view for awhile. But eventually the symptoms become visible to others. And, of course, our Owner knows precisely what goes on in these private relationships. For good reason a prerequisite for church leadership is the successful management of one's own family.[b] I want to lead by word and example like the good shepherds in Palestine. I don't need to throw stones.

---

a. 1 Pet. 5:3 b. 1 Tim. 3:4–5

You don't even know what will happen tomorrow.

—James 4:14

Adaptability and Decision Making

We began our journey considering the uniquely challenging environment in which herding takes place. Deserted areas with unpredictable rainfall, menacing predators, and a rugged terrain create major obstacles for a hungry and thirsty flock that moves slowly, wanders widely, and has no natural defenses. Along with environmental factors, a litany of economic, political, and social variables complicate many shepherds' existence. They must constantly renegotiate their positions as they eke out a living amid shifting sands and seasons in this ever-changing world. Adaptability, literally and figuratively, "goes with the territory."

The wilderness has historically been a forge for specific character traits. In a setting where "nothing can be depended on from year to year," where variability and unpredictability define the geographical and bioclimatic realities, opportunism and adaptability become key to survival and successful land use.[1] The desert becomes an incubator of innovation. "In short, the shepherd must see to it that the opportunities afforded by nature are not lost."[2]

It seems as though Bedouin live in a constant state of triage, continually weighing the benefits and risks of decisions that often dramatically impact their livelihood. One observer describes sixty categories of decisions that traditional shepherds make throughout the year, categories that are interrelated and affected by circumstances mostly outside of human control. These include decisions about camp formation and disbanding, migration (information gathering, destination, direction, timing, daily distance), flock management (grazing, watering, milking, care of young/sick, accounting, hiring of help for shearing), camp management (people, tasks, disputes), market interactions (information gathering, shearing, sheep and wool sales, to whom, when, at what rate), and external relations (interactions with the government and settled populations)—to name a few![3] In the words of Aref Abu-Rabiah, a Bedouin anthropologist, "The system of decision-making to meet the needs of the flock is a work of art spread over the entire year."[4]

I became quite impressed with the confident agility of the Bedouin, their nimble shifting from one role to another, synergistic response to rapid change, and willingness to move with less than a day's notice. The fluid existence of these shepherds reflects their core sense of attachment to their flocks, rather than to a specific geographical home.

This identity shapes their view of time as well as place, a perspective shared by Sarakatsani herders in the Southern Balkans:

> Time is not for the Sarakatsani a homogeneous medium, units of which may be saved or lost. In one aspect, it is a succession of activities concerned directly or indirectly with the flocks and determined by the ecological rhythms of the different seasons and the changing conditions of temperature, grass, and water...Time then is not a scale marking a linear progress, or a means of divining life into portions of work and leisure, it is a continuum of activity within the family and in the service of the flock.[5]

Adaptability becomes a way of life when shepherding is a way of life.[6]

I've come to appreciate how adaptable and opportunistic God is in Scripture. His plan for humans in the Garden of Eden was "interrupted" by human sin. But God swiftly put a preconceived contingency plan in place. Then when sin became intolerable he cleared the earth of its inhabitants and started again with Noah's family. Another revision. Story after story shows the Lord of the universe working in triage mode, responding creatively to threats to his plan.

By 1100 BC, kingship was a concession to a tribal confederacy obsessed with the desire for conventional leadership. Samuel knew that the request betrayed unbelief. Yet God showed his capacity to give them what they wanted while simultaneously creating an institution that would bring them the Messiah. That response is more than passive acquiescence. It is sovereign opportunism!

The stories of wilderness wandering provide vivid examples of the Divine Shepherd's flexibility. The most significant adaptation in the wilderness came as a result of rebellious unbelief. Numbers 13 and 14 record the twelve spies' report from their forty-day reconnaissance mission in the Promised Land. They realistically described the opportunities and threats: "We went into the land to which you sent us, and it *does* flow with milk and honey! *But* the people who live there are powerful, and the cities are fortified and very large."[a] Two spies courageously held out for God's promise, but by the next day the whole community festered in mutiny: "We should choose another leader and go back to Egypt."[b]

God's first response to this debacle was to suggest recreating the nation with Moses and the faithful few.[c] In a revised decision, he chose to let the people live, though barring that generation from the Promised Land. They would wait for forty years in the desert—one year for each day of the spies' exploration: "Your children will be shepherds here for forty years, suffering for your unfaithfulness, until the last

a. Num. 13:27–28 b. Num. 14:4 c. Cf. Num. 14:24

of your bodies lies in the desert."[a] That next generation would be given the chance to pick up the challenge where their parents failed.

The original itinerary to Sinai and to the borders of Canaan would have taken only a few weeks or months. But God adapted his plan to the condition of his flock, and they were now facing a forty-year sojourn. Yet, throughout these four decades God would show himself faithful. He stayed with them, modifying his agenda, bringing meaning to a time of waiting.[b] He voluntarily bound his identity to theirs.[c]

While God's gracious flexibility in the face of changing circumstances is prominent in this passage, he is still the undisputed decision maker. A group of Israelites had a change of heart and decided to go up to the now-forbidden land. In their presumption they left the presence of their Shepherd and faced inevitable defeat.[d] God had already adapted his plans and they now had to get in line with his revised timetable.

In *The Hidden World of the Pastor*, Ken Swetland describes a pastor who faced a rape case, a suicide, and a funeral all in one week...his *first* week of pastoral ministry.[7] Many of us smile grimly, understanding that unpredictability and interruption "just goes with the territory." No matter what form of ministry we're in, we roll with the unexpected and adjust our plans accordingly. The challenge is to make modifications without losing sight of the big picture. We want to be like Israel's Shepherd who altered his short-term plans but kept to his overall objective. Biblical opportunism accepts change and surprise as inevitable, but it cannot be swamped by it.

---

a. Num. 14:33 b. Deut. 8:1–5 c. Cf. Num. 14:13–19 d. Num. 14:39–45

We need a theology of interruptions and obstructions. Often we find ourselves trying to resolve them as quickly as possible and get on with our agenda, without regard for their potentially redemptive dimensions. Interruptions may be invitations. I mentioned the request for kingship earlier. Consider how central this institution was for the coming of the Anointed One, the Son of David. God engaged the challenge, co-opted the change, and unveiled a contingency plan that realized his long-term purposes. I wonder how many times we, like Samuel, can't get past the roadblock threatening "Plan A." He was right about God's ideal, but he didn't have the agility to recognize the value of "Plan B." He had a failure of imagination.

I have found myself in leadership roles often possessing such a strong sense of what *needs* to be done, what direction we *must* take, and *when* we need to move, that I can't appreciate alternative ways forward. Sometimes, I'm just not willing to wait forty years! I don't want to lose my strong sense of purpose, but I want the flexibility, agility, adaptability, and opportunism that I've seen among good shepherds. Especially *the* Good Shepherd.

Surely I am with you always, to the very end of the age.

—Matthew 28:20

Being There

◊ "The Mid-East is not the Mid-West." We say this to American groups visiting Israel to prepare them for the unique political dynamics of the region. However, the statement is also true when it comes to herding practice. Herd owners around the world certainly share similar tasks: feeding, watering, watching for illness, milking, shearing, and so on. But one difference is outstanding. In America's Mid-West you'll find shepherding resembles ranching: sheep are left to graze in vast fenced-in pastures. In the Middle East you'll never find fenced pastures; consequently, you'll never find a flock grazing without a shepherd.

As we've observed in our journey, sheep scatter without a shepherd. They run when they sense danger. Their only hope for protection comes from the shepherd's presence. A flock outside in a desert night is helpless unless their shepherd is among them. The donkey can serve as an emergency surrogate only because it is equated with the shepherd.

The bonding that occurs as a result of round-the-clock care is remarkable. Sheep will follow the shepherd who personally provides, protects, and guides. This interpersonal history of frequent, long-term, and intimate contact secures the flock's obedience, even in times of great distress. A cycle of shepherd service and flock trust repeats and reinforces itself throughout the seasons.

The "you are with me" assurance of God's personal presence in The Shepherd Psalm runs like a golden thread throughout Scripture. God asked Abraham to give up his permanent home, inheritance, and family identity, with nothing more than promises to sustain his faith. The most important promise was, "I will be with you,"[a] a refrain repeated to his grandson Jacob.[b] While Abraham's descendents languished in Egyptian slavery, they questioned the credibility of this promise. But God raised up a shepherd to lead them out of bondage. His promise to Moses was the same: "I will be with you."[c]

For forty years God was personally present for his people in the very physical phenomenon of cloud and fire. Their Divine Shepherd never abandoned them in the wilderness, though at one point Moses feared being left to lead alone. He said, "You have been telling me, 'Lead these people,' but you have not let me know whom you will send with me."

His ever-patient, ever-present Lord replied, "My Presence will go with you, and I will give you rest."

This reassured Moses, but he still posed a condition: "If your Presence does not go with us, do not send us up from here."[d]

God reminded David of his sustaining and empowering personal presence after he had settled into his role as king of Israel: "I took you from the pasture and from following the flock to be ruler over my people Israel. *I have been with you wherever you have gone*, and I have cut off all your enemies from before you. Now I will make your name great."[e]

---

a. Gen. 26:3 b. Gen. 31:3 c. Exod. 3:12 d. Exod. 33:12–15 e. 2 Sam. 7:8–9

The promise of God's presence materialized in the divine Son of David, Jesus Christ. One of his messianic titles, *Immanuel*, means "God with us."[a] Jesus gave the world unmediated access to God's holy presence. John's gospel says, literally, "The Divine Word was embodied and tented among us."[b] Jesus is identified here with the Divine Shepherd who had tented with Israel and led them in such spectacular and personal ways.[c]

As the Messiah prepared to leave his disciples, he restated the foundational promise: "I will ask the Father, and He will give you another Helper, *that He may be with you forever.*"[d] This Helper was God's own Spirit, the ever-present evidence of God's presence. In his final commission in Matthew 28:19–20 Jesus sent his followers out to disciple the nations, making the promise permanent: "Surely I am with you always, to the very end of the age."

When I first heard a leadership consultant use the phrase "Leadership By Walking Around" (LBWA), I didn't take it seriously. It sounded like a lack of leadership. However, leading by personal presence or "walking around,"[1] is now a recognized element of effective leadership in business and education. Regular, informal exposure to the people who work for you yields good decision making and boosts productivity. This exposure is not passive proximity but attentive, responsive listening—an engagement of all the senses to discover what *really* matters in the lives of your help. LBWA recognizes that leaders cannot understand their workers unless they spend quantity and quality time among them. We might simply call this principle, "being there leadership."

This principle resonates with the biblical passages we've investigated. In particular, it restates what Jesus did so effectively with his disciples. Everything else

---

a. Isa. 7:14; Matt. 1:23 b. John 1:14 (author's translation) c. 2 Sam. 7:6 d. John 14:16 (NASB)

he did to train them was predicated on his predictable, attentive presence among them.

This principle is as true for a parent as for a pastor.

I've seen a wonderful example of "being there leadership" in a school that our children attend. From the school's inception, the headmaster, "Mr. T.," made it a habit to greet the students every day when they stepped out of their cars. Apparently this had been his practice even when he led a school previously with five thousand students! Mr. T.'s smiling presence communicates welcome, acceptance, and interest. He returns calls and letters personally. His door is open for students, staff, and parents, regardless of the concern. On any given day you might see Mr. T. walking around, using his senses to discern all the elements that make up a school's atmosphere.

To make personal presence a priority, Mr. T. has had to make some significant choices in his schedule. He arrives at school usually by 5:30 AM to take care of important management tasks. And he does stay late on many nights.

Mr. T. makes a vital leadership choice every day by being available. You trust a person like that. Even if some projects don't get done and some objectives aren't reached. People feel valued when they are given personal time and attention.

I'd like to end our reflections with the promise of Jesus to be with us forever. That oath was made to a group that would take his mission across the globe, an immense task that could only be commissioned with a pledge of personal presence. Paul sensed that God was a "fellow-worker" in the gospel.[a] When we reach out in God's service, he is beside us, "walking around."

No fences.

Simply the powerful pull of personal presence. The Spirit of the Good Shepherd leading us with a secure guarantee that he always will.

---

a. 1 Thes. 3:2

And I will dwell in the house of the LORD forever.

—Psalm 23:6

Home

One brilliantly clear winter day our family rode camels to a remote Bedouin campsite in Wadi Rum in southern Jordan. Although my daughter was thrown from her cantankerous mount early in the day, we all arrived safely at dusk, ready for a rustic meal sizzling on the open fire. We removed our shoes and crossed the blanket threshold that guaranteed our safety and provision in the tent of our host. Unfortunately, as the fire's embers faded, so did the usually dazzling stars. A rapidly moving storm front had arrived in the valley. Wailing wind began to shake the tents as snow whirled around us. Concerned for our safety should the tent collapse, our hosts radioed in a Land Rover to execute a rapid exit from the desert. Though our adventure was aborted, a basic truth about tent dwelling became obvious.

Home for the Bedouin is a tent on poles, secured only by ropes and a handful of stakes. The tent is typically made of between six and eight woven goat-hair panels sewn together. The natural fiber is warm and waterproof. It is easily rolled up to catch a breeze or staked down to keep out the sand and sun. With frequent patching, a tent might last from fifteen to twenty years. The more wealthy desert dwellers have large tents that can serve guests and, if necessary, needy animals. To have an "enlarged tent" is a sign of prosperity.[a] Of the most worthwhile possessions in life, the Bedouin list "a tent spread wide" as number one.[1]

Though these "houses of hair" with their "pillars" are central to Bedouin life and their legendary hospitality, the tent is a simple and fragile structure. Hanging blankets create rooms; pillows form the furniture. The pastoralists' homes reflect their transient, vulnerable, and ephemeral existence; their life is "a tent-pole on a camel."[2] Their fabric dwellings can be wrapped up and loaded on camels or trucks within a couple of hours. And they can collapse instantly in a storm.

Archaeologists find little material evidence of pastoralists from antiquity. Most evidence has vanished in the wind. The most significant remains of transient people groups are their relationships and the stories that secure their identities.

When I read the New Testament I'm struck by how many times Abraham is mentioned. I've come to appreciate one of the reasons why. Like many pastoralists today, Abraham was a tent dweller. This cultural reality matched his spiritual identity: "By faith he lived as an alien in the land of promise, as in a foreign land, dwelling in tents with Isaac and Jacob, fellow heirs of the same promise."[b] Abraham was a temporary resident, sojourning in this world. Like Bedouin today, his mobility was "irreducibly constitutive of his identity."[3]

Abraham's transient lifestyle was to become an essential element of Israel's identity when they settled in the Promised Land. Those contributing a gift of firstfruits were to make a confession that aligned themselves with their faith-filled ancestor. They began with the words, "My father was a wandering Aramean."[c] The Hebrew word for wandering suggests that he was a fugitive of sorts in this world.

a. Isa. 54:2 b. Heb. 11:9 (NASB) c. Deut. 26:5

The Bible also describes God as a tent dweller. One of Israel's pilgrimage holidays was *Sukkot*, the Festival of Tabernacles. In the seventh month of each year, every family was to leave their stone homes and to camp outside

in tents for a week. *Sukkot* was a regular ritual reminder of God's provision in the wilderness when he camped with them. It reactivated their identity as a pilgrim people.[4]

In fact, God was a *contented* tent dweller. When David expressed his desire to build a permanent temple befitting his Lord's honor, the response was surprising: "I have not dwelt in a house since the day I brought up the sons of Israel from Egypt, even to this day; *but I have been moving about in a tent, even in a tabernacle.*"[a] In this passage David was informed that God had never asked for a "house of cedar."

At a time when King David was ready to enjoy the stability of settled life, God inserted a reminder that stationary permanence was not the divine ideal. This important lesson was also for the community that would one day forfeit its temple—only to discover that God could dwell among them again in the wilderness of exile.

---

a. 2 Sam. 7:6 (NASB)

When the Messiah Jesus came, he literally "tented" among his people.[a] To a prospective disciple Jesus warned, "Foxes have holes and birds of the air have nests, but the Son of Man has no place to lay his head."[b] His real home was in heaven, and he never lost sight of it. Paul, the Syrian tentmaker, reflected the same transient view of his body when he said, "Now we know that if the earthly tent we live in is destroyed, we have a building from God, an eternal house in heaven, not built by human hands."[c]

Hebrews 11 exonerates a host of biblical saints who did not receive the promises they were assured during their lifetimes. The prime example is Abraham, but others also "admitted that they were aliens and strangers on earth."[d] Many "went about in sheepskins and goatskins, destitute, persecuted and mistreated—the world was not worthy of them. They wandered in deserts and mountains, and in caves and holes in the ground."[e]

What a profound thought: The world is not worthy of those who do not consider it their home. With their spiritual father Abraham, these faithful pilgrims look forward to their truly permanent home, "the city with foundations, whose architect and builder is God."[f]

In his vision of heaven John hears a loud voice crying, "Behold, the tabernacle of God is among men, and He will dwell among them, and they shall be

a. John 1:14 b. Matt. 8:20 c. 2 Cor. 5:1 (cf. 2 Pet. 1:13–14) d. Heb. 11:13 e. Heb. 11:37–38 f. Heb. 11:10

His people, and God Himself will be among them."[a] The heavenly *city*, ironically, is the *tent* of the Divine Shepherd.

The identity of temporary resident needs to be imprinted on our own minds as leaders. We need to know personally that our true home is in heaven and that this earth is simply a place where we promote God's interests. As we build buildings and make long-term plans, we easily forget how transient and ephemeral our lives and ministries really are. Have we forgotten that we are "a mist that appears for a little while and then vanishes"?[b]

While we need to pursue objectives, goals, and strategic plans for our communities, the ultimate goal is to *get them all home*. We will fail if they are so distracted by the seemingly permanent items of our experience that they forget what is eternal. Are we leading people with a sense of this world's transience and heaven's permanence? Do we give evidence in our own behavior that what counts for *us* is what's ahead? Are we leading our flocks intentionally along the edges of settled society—where citizens of this world root their identity—moving them forward to their permanent home? We're headed for the tent of God where we will dwell forever.

a. Rev. 21:3 (NASB) b. James 4:14

*And when the Chief Shepherd appears, you will
receive the crown of glory that will never fade away.*

—1 Peter 5:4

Epilogue

What will you do when you go back to America? What will you remember about us? Will you forget us? Sleeping on the ground, grazing sheep, eating food cooked on open fires, riding camels, walking with our animals...What will remind you of us once you have left, about our life of constant travel? You said you will write... on our life and ways...How will this be of use...?[1]

W hat *will* we remember about the shepherds who have opened their tents to us? Will we remember most their stories of wolves and years of drought? Or how they find water and heal their sick? Will we forget how hard their work is and how transient their existence?

We cannot fully comprehend the life and work of people from another culture. More challenging and relevant is the task of allowing insights from this culture to illuminate what Scripture teaches us about leadership. The real work of transforming lies before us. Our journaling has just begun.

As we take a final pause and consider these days we've spent together, I am personally reminded of how comprehensive shepherding is. From loading wool on trucks to looking for the lost in caverns. From making milk products to securing safe pens. From gentle midwifery to stern discipline. This diversity is just as striking in the world of spiritual shepherds. We need to be as effective at the sickbed as in the boardroom. As articulate in the pulpit as in the city council meeting. As attentive in a counseling session as we are just "walking around." We need integrity at the office and integrity at home.

I've been impressed in this journey by the many creative tensions in shepherd leadership. We've been called to self-sacrifice as well as to self-care, to be wise leaders while following humbly, to have determination with adaptability, to be physically present but skilled at delegating, to work alone and to work together.

The title *While Shepherds Watch Their Flocks* has gathered layers of meaning along the way. Although shepherds appear to be idly staring at their flocks, they are mentally active. Watching requires attentiveness. They are processing the variables of the ever-changing environment.

While shepherds watch their flocks, predators watch them too. Watching requires vigilance in the presence of other often-concealed watchers. While spiritual shepherds watch their flocks, their Heavenly Shepherd watches over them. We have a Sleepless Shepherd whom we can trust while we sleep.

Finally, while shepherds watch their flocks, the flocks are watching them. Peter encourages elders to be model shepherds, "examples for the flock."[a] The apostle asked three times by the Chief Shepherd to "feed my sheep" has suggested yet one more paradox: Good shepherds raise sheep to become fellow shepherds.

---

a. 1 Pet. 5:3

Endnotes

Introduction

1. Spoken by Riaka shepherds from western Rajasthan in India. Cited by Arun Agrawal, *Greener Pastures* (Durham, NC: Duke University, 1999), 1.
2. Though times and customs change, there is a remarkably resilient set of practices and perspectives common among pastoralists.
3. Bedouin (both singular and plural) are the native tribal groups in the Middle East. First references to the "Bedu" come from Ebla in the third millennium BC. Of the four to five million Bedouin people living today, only about 10 percent live in the traditional ways described in this book.

Day 1: Wilderness

1. Lady Anne Blunt, *Bedouin Tribes of the Euphrates* (New York: Harper & Brothers, 1879), 340.
2. Clinton Bailey, *A Culture of Survival* (New Haven: Yale University, 2004), 19.
3. Kay Shirley, *The Bedouin* (New York: Crane, Russak, 1978), 36.
4. P. Marcel Kurpershoek, ed., *Oral Poetry and Narratives From Central Asia*, vol. 1 (Leiden: E. J. Brill, 1994), 139.
5. Jibrail S. Jabbur, *The Bedouins and the Desert* (New York: State University, 1995), 50–51.
6. Elijah would come back to this same mountain when he needed a word from God.
7. This onomatopoetic Hebrew phrase is taken from Genesis 1:2.

Day 3: Called to Care

1. Pastoralism describes the work of people-groups (i.e. pastoralists) whose primary source of subsistence and/or production comes from flocks and herd animals.
2. Another pastor in Israel shared how as a goat herder God called him into ministry. The vision he had at that time was of people serving the needy out of an oasis tent. He now leads "Tents of Mercy," a congregation that lives up to this vision by caring for immigrants and the poor.

Day 4: Streams in the Desert

1. Kurpershoek, *Oral Poetry*, 107–109.

2. God promised such a flood when the Israelites were attacking Moab in the wilderness of Edom: "You will see neither wind nor rain, yet this valley will be filled with water" (2 Kgs. 3:17).

3. Emanuel Marx, "Oases in South Sinai," *Human Ecology* 27, no. 2 (1999): 345.

4. Bailey, *A Culture*, 32. See Job's comparison of deceptive friends to "torrents of wadis which vanish" (Job 6:15 NASB).

Day 5: Spring Up O Well

1. For pictures of well chains see Michael Evanari, Leslie Shanan, & Naphtali Tadmore, *The Negev* (Harvard: Harvard University, 1971).

2. Alois Musil, *Manners and Customs of the Rwala Bedouin* (New York: American Geographical Society, 1928), 676–684. Cf. William and Fidelity Lancaster, "Limitations on Sheep and Goat Herding in the Eastern Badia of Jordan," *Levant* 28, 1991: 128.

3. Evanari, 1971. Note that Uzziah made many cisterns in the Negev (2 Chron. 26:10).

4. Exod. 15:22–27; Prov. 25:25-26; Ezek. 34:18-19; James 3:11–12.

5. Nancie L. Gonzalez, ed., "Social and Technological Management in Dry Lands," *AAAS Selected Symposium* 10 (1978): 118.

6. Jabbur, 408.

7. Beer Sheva can also mean "Seven Wells." Bedouin say there are only five wells that do not dry up in the Negev, most of them near Beer Sheva. In the whole Negev region there are only true perennial watercourses at Ein Avdat and Kadesh Barnea. See Emmanuel Marx, *Bedouin of the Negev* (Manchester: Manchester University, 1967), 24–25.

8. This story is recounted in Exodus 2.

9. God "turned the rock into a pool, the *hard rock* into springs of water" (Ps. 114:8).

Day 6: Greener Pastures

1. To conserve land, the *Hima* system designates fields in the following ways: for fodder, limited grazing for some animals, grazing for limited seasons, grazing during drought, protected for wild flora and fauna. See John Shoup, "Middle Eastern Sheep Pastoralism and the Hima System" in John G. Galaty & Douglas L. Johnson, eds., *World of Pastoralism* (New York: Guilford Press, 1990), 195–215.

2. This was the distance Ruth's adopted family traveled when they left famine-ravaged Bethlehem for Moab.

3. Sometimes the greener grass is someone else's land—another farmer's or open land occupied by others first. See Job 24:2: "Some remove the landmarks; They seize and devour flocks." Pasture stealing is as much a threat as sheep stealing.

4. P. Marcel Kurpershoek, ed., *Bedouin Poets of the Dawasir Tribe*, vol. 17 (Leiden: E. J. Brill, 1999), 39, 172–73.

5. Ibid., 178–9.

6. The two most common Hebrew words for wilderness (*midbar* and *naweh*) refer to grazing areas.

7. Joan Westenholz (2004), "The Good Shepherd" in *Melammu Symposia* 4, eds., A. Panaino & A. Piras (Milano: University of Bologna, 2004), 167.

8. Ibid., 167.

Day 7: Feed My Sheep

1. Lancaster, 128.

2. Joseph J. Hobbs, *Bedouin Life in the Egyptian Wilderness* (Austin: University of Texas, 1989).

3. Shemot Rabbah 2:2

4. 1 Tim. 4:6 (NASB). Paul uses the word *hugiaino* for *healthy* teaching and faith in 1 Tim. 1:10; 4:6; Tit. 1:9, 13; 2:1, 2, 8.

Day 8: The Shepherd Healer

1. Yann Arthus-Bertrand, "Portland Ram and Friend," ‹www.jannarthusbertrand. com›, accessed January, 2006.

2. Dalal Khalil Safadi & Victoria Safadi Basha, *A Thousand and One Arabic Proverbs* (Beirut: American Press, 1954), 26.

3. Barbara Smith, Mark Aseltine, & Gerald Kennedy, *Beginning Shepherd's Manual*, 2d ed. (Ames, IA: Iowa State University, 1997), 71.

4. Phillip Keller, *A Shepherd Looks at Psalm 23* (Grand Rapids: Zondervan, 1970), 115.

Day 9: Midwives & Nurses

Lead verse in author's translation

1. John Kennedy Campbell, *Honour, Family, and Patronage* (Oxford: Clarendon, 1964), 27–28.

2. "Sheep Become Less Agitated When Shown a Friendly Face," ‹www.spectator. co.uk ›, accessed Dec. 15, 2001.

3. Faddoul Moghabghab, The *Shepherd Song on the Hills of Lebanon* (New York: E. P. Dutton, 1907), 107.

4. The Hebrew literally reads "from behind the ewes," implying that he was going at their pace with a caring eye on them.

5. The Hebrew verb used here, *nakhah* (to gently lead), will be explored in Day 29.

Day 10: Lost and Found

Lead verse in author's translation
1. Moghabghab, 77–79.
2. See S. C. Barton, 'Parables of God's Love and Forgiveness' in R. N. Longenecker (ed.), *The Challenge of Jesus' Parables* (Grand Rapids: Eerdmans, 2000), 205.
3. Cf. Jim Henderson, *a.k.a. Lost* (New York: WaterBrook, 2005).
4. The Joshua Project, ‹www.joshuaproject. net›, accessed March 10, 2013. See the Center for the Study of Global Christianity at www.gordonconwell. edu for the world's most sophisticated religion data base.

Day 11: Gathering the Scattered

1. From this important image we retain the word "Diaspora" for people separated from their homeland.
2. Numbers 27:17; I Kings 22:17. This is a refrain in the *Lament for Ur* after the ancient city's destruction.
3. Merodach-baladan II (Westenholz, 173–4).

4. See Luke 15:1, the setting for the Lost Sheep parable.

Day 12: Satisfaction and Restoration

1. As small ruminants, sheep and goats constantly re-chew the food they process through four stomachs.
2. I'm reminded of two brothers mentioned in Gen. 4:20; Jabal, the "father of those who live in tents and raise livestock," and his brother, Jubal, "the father of all who play the harp and flute."
3. *shuv*
4. The Hebrew verb for restoration and refreshment, *hayah*, means to "return to life"!
5. A literal translation of the Hebrew term *menukhot*.
6. Author's translation. Most translations don't capture the inner-biblical allusions Mark is intent on making.

Day 13: The Staff

Lead verse in author's translation
1. Keller, 100.
2. Ibid., 101.

Day 14: Named and Known

Lead verse in author's translation

1. Agrawal, 21–22.
2. See Jer. 33:13. Though many groups in Jordan do not name each of their flock, it is common in other regions. See H. R. P. Dickson, *Arabs of the Desert* (London: George Allen & Unwin, 1949, 1951), 402–403. It was obviously so in Jesus' day (John 10:3).
3. Dickson, 403–4 (italics added). This naming and knowledge is typical of 'Awazim tribes of Kuwait and Najd.
4. This owner is atypical in his self-imposed standards of daily involvement. More commonly, shepherding is left in the hands of the youngest in the family with parental supervision. This was probably the case for David in his younger years.

Day 15: Protection

Lead verse in author's translation
1. Campbell, 26.
2. Richard Critchfield, *The Golden Bowl be Broken* (Bloomington, ID: Indiana University, 1973), 28.
3. Daniel David Luckenbill, *Ancient Records of Assyria and Babylon* I (Chicago: University of Chicago, 1926), 39.
4. Hammurabi wrote, "I made the peoples rest in friendly habitations, I did not let them have anyone to terrorize them." Cf. James B. Pritchard, ed., *Ancient Near Eastern Texts Relating to the Old Testament* (Princeton: Princeton University, 1969), 177-178 (hereafter ANET).

Day 16: While Shepherds Watch Their Flocks

Lead verse in author's translation
1. This phrase, coined by astronaut Frank Borman after the Apollo I fire in 1967, is used to explain the behavior of the CIA and FBI in the wake of national tragedies like "9/11."
2. In I Sam. 17:20 David supplies his brothers in Saul's armies, leaving the family flock in the hands of a "guard" (same word).
3. Author's translation. The same verb *gregoreo* (to be alert, awake, watchful) is used also in I Pet. 5:8 with reference to the roaring devil.

Day 17: Recognizing the Wolves

1. Richard Tapper, *Pasture and Politics* (London: Academic, 1979), 91.
2. John Lewis Burkhardt, *Arabic Proverbs* (London: Curzon, 1984), 10.
3. Jabbur, 85.
4. Another proverb opines, "The goatherd gets gray long before he's old, from

chasing the wolf all night from the fold" (Bailey, *A Culture*, 34).

5. David Outerbridge, *The Last Shepherds* (New York: Viking, 1979), 22.

6. Critchfield, 23. This quote originally referred to hyenas but it applies equally well to the sentiments felt for wolves.

7. Babylonian Talmud Mezi'a 7:8–9.

8. I know of different cases where the pastor's children—both boys and girls— were molested. Another pastor friend's wife was raped by an elder when he was away on a trip. Unfortunately, cases of molestation and rape by church leaders are all too common.

Day 18: Facing the Lions

Lead verse in author's translation

1. Safadi, 34.

2. William W. Hallo, ed., *The Context of Scripture*, vols. 1–3 (Leiden: E. J. Brill, 1997-), vol. 2, 301.

3. C. S. Lewis' fictitious demonic figure "Screwtape" discloses a common objective to his apprentice Wormwood: "To us a human is primarily food; our aim is *the absorption of its will* into ours..." (C. S. Lewis, *Screwtape Letters*, [San Francisco: HarperSanFrancisco, 1942, 1996], 38, italics added).

4. The temple to the Greek god Pan at Caesarea-Philippi was located in front of a huge rock face (covered with idol niches) and next to a cave where one of the sources of the Jordan River emerged. Considered an opening into Hades, human sacrifices were thrown into this cave. The "rock" on which Jesus promises to build his church may be this temple site—the epitome of pagan worship.

5. Lewis, 5.

6. Jesus wins the great war against Satan with a sword coming out of his mouth (Rev. 1:16; 2:16; 19:15, 21).

Day 19: The Other Lion

1. See my discussion of *your people* and *my people* in the Moses narratives in Timothy S. Laniak, *Shepherds After My Own Heart* (Downers Grove, IL: InterVarsity, 2006), 88–90.

2. Daniel Chanan Matt, trans., *Zohar* (Ramsey, NJ: Paulist, 1983), 58.

3. C. S. Lewis, *The Lion, The Witch, and the Wardrobe* (New York: Macmillan, 1950, 1970), 75–76.

Day 20: Gatekeepers

1. Ancient King Sargon II described a defeated commander who "fled alone

like a shepherd whose flock is robbed."
(Hallo, vol. 2, 293). Cf. Job 1:14–15.

2. Outerbridge, 104.

3. Jabbur, 415.

Day 21: Dogs

1. Some people referred to themselves as dogs in a deliberately self-deprecating manner (2 Sam. 9:8; 2 Kgs. 8:13).

2. A dog is Tobit's companion in the apocryphal book named after him (Tob. 6:2; 11:4). The Egyptian text, *Instruction of Any* (c. 1000 BC), might also have a loyal pet in mind: "The dog obeys the word, and walks behind its master" (Hallo, vol. 1, 114).

3. Hallo, vol. 2, 113.

4. Dave Grossman, ‹www. gleamingedge.com/mirrors/ onsheepwolvesandsheepdogs.html›, accessed March 10, 2013.

Day 22: Justice

1. Westenholz, 171.

2. ANET, 164.

Day 23: The Rod

Lead verse in author's translation

1. Author's translation differs from others which read either "*break* them with a *rod* of iron" (NASB) or "*rule* them with an iron *scepter*" (NIV). The verbal form in this phrase could reflect either of two similar roots, one meaning *break* and the other *shepherd/rule*. The use of the term *rod* (*shevet*) with the verb *to shepherd* (*ra'ah*) makes the most sense. The Septuagint (Greek Old Testament) translates the verse as I do, as does John in Rev. 12:5 and 19:15.

2. J. P. J. Olivier, "The Sceptre of Justice and Ps. 45:7b," *Journal of Northwest Semitic Languages* 7 (1979): 48.

Day 24: A Living Sacrifice

1. From the hymn, "There is a Fountain."

2. Tradition tells us that after Peter was severely scourged and crucified in Nero's Rome, he was hung upside down at his own request. See W. Grinton Berry, ed., *Foxe's Book of Martyrs* (Grand Rapids: Spire, 1998), 12.

3. Josef Ton, *Suffering, Martyrdom, and Rewards in Heaven* (New York: University Press of America, 1997) xvi.

4. The classic text on martyrdom in the history of the Church is *Foxe's Book of Martyrs* noted above. For a study of recent martyrdom, see the second edition of James and Marty Hefli, *By Their Blood: Christian Martyrs of the Twentieth Century* (Grand Rapids: Baker, 2004).

5. Regarding his own death Jesus had made this point, "Unless a kernel of wheat falls to the ground and dies, it remains only a single seed. But if it dies, it produces many seeds" (John 12:24).

Day 25: Darkness

1. John 9:40–41. The word "blind" is used fourteen times in chapter 9 and then again, after the Good Shepherd parable, in John 10:21.
2. See E. Allison Peers, ed. and trans., *Dark Night of the Soul by Saint John of the Cross*, 3 ed. (Garden City, NY: Doubleday, 1959).

Day 26: Guard Yourselves

Lead verse in NASB
1. Lois Beck, "Herd Owners and Hired Shepherds," *Ethnology* 19, no. 3 (1980): 338.
2. Tomas J. Barfield, *The Central Asian Arabs of Afghanistan* (Austin: University of Texas, 1981), 58.
3. Peter warns shepherds of the church to work willingly, "...*not greedy for money*, but eager to serve" (1 Pet. 5:2). Earlier in this letter he mentions a group who hasn't followed his advice: "In their greed these teachers will exploit you with stories they have made up" (2 Pet. 2:3). See also Titus 1:11.

Day 27: My Sleepless Shepherd

1. Hallo, vol. 1, 564.
2. Critchfield, 27.

Day 28: Guidance

Lead verse in author's translation
1. Critchfield, 28–29.
2. This phrase was coined in *Shepherds After My Own Heart* (Laniak, 22).

Day 29: Following The Leader

1. This term, for example, can describe people driven into exile (Deut. 4:27; Isa. 20:4).
2. The single Greek verb *odegeo* is frequently used to convey these different meanings in the Septuagint and in the New Testament. This verb describes the Spirit's role as guide in the believer's life (John 16:13).

Day 30: Righteous Ruts

1. Revised from a July 8, 2005 Associated Press web news release.
2. *tsalmavet*.

Day 31: Working Together

Lead verse in author's translation

1. r'h
2. Frederick Baker, *The Last Shepherds of the Abruzzi* (Hertfordshire: Baracca, 1989), 12 (quoting Paul Rowinski).
3. Paul's notion of ministry is shaped by sharing. Using the Greek prefix *syn*, he refers to his epistle readers as fellow elders, fellow heirs, fellow servants, fellow prisoners, fellow workers, fellow slaves, fellow citizens, fellow soldiers, fellow partakers, and fellow members of the body.

Day 32: Indigenous Leadership

Lead verse in author's translation

Day 33: Productivity

1. For documentation for the numbers in this paragraph, see Laniak, 42–46.
2. Until the time of David wool was plucked.
3. Outerbridge, 21.
4. Gideon Kressel, *Let Shepherding Endure* (Albany: NY State University, 2003), 126.

Day 33: Productivity

Lead verse in NASB

1. Hallo, vol. 1, 44.
2. Deut. 7:13; 28:4, 18, 31, 51. Job had a flock of 7,000 destroyed by Satan, but God rewarded him in the end with 14,000.
3. Nahum M. Sarna, *The JPS Commentary: Genesis* (Philadelphia: Jewish Publication Society, 1989), 212. Cf. Scott B. Noegel, "Sex, Sticks, and the Trickster in Gen. 30:31–43," *Journal of Ancient Near Eastern Society* 25 (1997): 7–17.
4. See Nogah Harouveni, *Desert and Shepherd in Our Biblical Heritage* (Lod, Israel: Neot Kedumim, 1991).

Day 35: Think Flock

1. Donald Powell Cole, *Bedouin, Settlers, and Holiday Makers* (Cairo: American University, 1998), 129.
2. For more detail, see Laniak, 43.
3. It is likely that the original meaning of the Hebrew word for "people" (*'am*) is "flock."

Day 36: Finding Good Help

1. Beck, 337.
2. Tapper, 101.
3. Barfield, 58

4. Beck, 331.
5. Laniak, 248
6. One of the character requirements for elders is freedom from the love of money (1 Tim. 3:3).

Day 37: Authority and Abuse

Lead verse in NASB
1. Lynn Anderson, *They Smell Like Sheep* (West Monroe, LS, 1997), 29–30.
2. The word *perek* is used elsewhere only in Exod. 1:13–14 and in prohibitions against slavery in God's freed community (Lev. 25: 43, 46, 53).

Day 38: Adaptability

1. Lancaster, *Limitations*, p 128
2. Roy H. Behnke, *The Herders of Cyrenaica* (Urbana, IL: University of Illinois, 1980), 36.
3. Agrawal, 133.
4. Aref Abu-Rabiah, *The Negev Bedouin and Livestock Rearing* (Oxford: Berg, 1994), 3.
5. Campbell, 34.
6. The Sarakatsani say, "Shepherding has intrinsic value; it is a way of life, not merely one way of remaining alive" (ibid.).

7. Kenneth L. Swetland, *The Hidden World of the Pastor* (Grand Rapids: Baker, 1995), 24.

Day 39: Being There

1. Robert Waterman, *In Search of Excellence* (New York: Harper & Row, 1982).

Day 40: Home

1. Clinton Bailey, *Bedouin Poetry from Sinai and the Negev* (Oxford: Clarendon, 1991), 138.
2. Bailey, *A Culture*, 30.
3. Agrawal, 20.
4. The Rechabites (Jeremiah 35) were a community that retained a semi-nomadic pastoral lifestyle, reminding the rest of the community of their roots.

Epilogue

1. Agrawal, 167.

Notes

Notes

Notes

Notes

Notes

Notes

David Ormesher
Photographer

When he's not tramping around the world as an intrepid photographer and serving as chairman of Global Relief and Development Partners, David Ormesher is in his office as CEO of a leading branding and relationship marketing agency called closerlook, inc. He is a graduate of Wheaton College and lives with his wife and three children in Chicago, Illinois.

While Shepherds Watch Their Flocks is available directly from
www.shepherdleader.com,
a site dedicated to providing resources that support
today's shepherds in their various ministries.

You'll find another foundational resource by Tim Laniak,
*Shepherds After My Own Heart: Pastoral Traditions
and Leadership in the Bible* (IVP, 2006),
along with forums in "The Tent" to discuss your journey through these two books.

Supporting resources include image collections, posters, staffs, rods, and more.

Dates for upcoming leadership-focused experiential tours of the
Middle East are listed on www.shepherdleader.com.